I0797954

HIDDEN
FLOWERS

A MEMOIR

HIDDEN FLOWERS

KEIKO HONDA

Copyright © 2025 Keiko Honda

All rights reserved. No part of this publication may be reproduced, stored in a retrieval system, or transmitted in any form or by any means—electronic, mechanical, audio recording, or otherwise—without the written permission of the publisher or a licence from Access Copyright, Toronto, Canada.

Heritage House Publishing Company Ltd.
heritagehouse.ca

Cataloguing information available from Library and Archives Canada
978-1-77203-560-5 (paperback)
978-1-77203-561-2 (e-book)

Edited by Claire Mulligan
Proofread by Nandini Thaker
Cover and interior book design by Setareh Ashrafologhalai
Cover image: *Floating Free* by Keiko Honda
Interior images by Keiko Honda unless otherwise indicated
Image dimensions are in inches, expressed as width × height
Pattern designs by Setareh Ashrafologhalai

The interior of this book was produced on FSC®-certified, acid-free paper, processed chlorine free, and printed with vegetable-based inks.

Heritage House gratefully acknowledges that the land on which we live and work is within the traditional territories of the lək̓ʷəŋən (Esquimalt and Songhees), Malahat, Pacheedaht, Scia'new, T'Sou-ke, and W̱SÁNEĆ (Pauquachin, Tsartlip, Tsawout, Tseycum) Peoples.

We acknowledge the financial support of the Government of Canada through the Canada Book Fund (CBF) and the Canada Council for the Arts, and the Province of British Columbia through the British Columbia Arts Council and the Book Publishing Tax Credit.

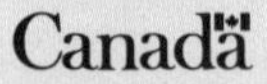

29 28 27 26 25 1 2 3 4 5

Printed in China

*To my perennially
blossoming daughter, Maya.*

*May you bloom in your
own unique way.*

*With my deepest love
and admiration.*

PENSIVE
watercolour,
9 × 12

I painted a portrait of my daughter from a photo, which appears accidentally more mature and pensive than she was at that age. Perhaps this painting gives me a glimpse of her future self, a vision of the woman she is becoming. Or, perhaps, it gives a truer sense of her inner self. Maybe it's not an accident at all.

CONTENTS

FROST
watercolour,
5 × 7

My tiny Japanese rock garden's pond is frozen, making a beautiful imprint of winter foliage. A frozen still life. The ice preserves the delicate shapes of leaves, a winter's gift. Soon the thaw will come, and the imprint will vanish.

INTRODUCTION

IN MY DEBUT MEMOIR, *Accidental Blooms*, I described inventing—perhaps it was more a process of discovering—a kind of rebirth following a crisis that left me paralyzed from the chest down. This transformation was helped greatly by encounters with new people and new experiences. In that narrative, my emerging identity, my work, and my role as a mother all revolved around my newborn daughter, Maya. It resembled a dance in which I was following an invisible partner; that is, until I started to choreograph my own movement.

My new memoir starts where the first one ended, when I was guiding Maya through the process of applying to university, and when I was fearing the day that I would lose her. Here in these pages, I navigate new, complex, intergenerational cultural challenges, nurturing a new romantic relationship that defies easy categorization, and preparing what I hope will ultimately be both a legacy and a creative act.

During this time of radical change, I looked for an aesthetic metaphor for self-transformation. I was drawn to a book called *Fushikaden* (*The Flowering Spirit*) by Zeami Motokiyo, a fourteenth-century master of Noh, an ancient form of Japanese theatre. In it, he explores how to perfect one's art within the context of constant flux. Within this masterpiece, I found valuable insights for my own process of self-discovery.

Zeami teaches how to create the most powerful artistic experience through indirection and subtlety by choosing the ripest moment for the artistic creation to flower. This resonated deeply with me. Here, he half reveals the secret: "If it is hidden, it is the flower." While there are various interpretations, I believe he is enticing us to nurture a flower that blooms throughout one's life. There are seeds and seasons that continue to develop year after year. And so, might we meet that flower again? As a middle-aged woman in her late fifties, whose child-rearing duties are freshly complete, I wonder what kind of flower I want to nurture, and if I can bloom at all. Looking back on my daughter's departure, I realize it was a profoundly unsettling and unfamiliar experience. Yet, I am beginning to see that her leaving is illuminating a new path for me in ways I had never imagined. As I experiment with ways of blooming, I hope that readers will find some value in my at times chaotic ventures, and that they will discover the transformative power of the hidden flower metaphor in their own lives.

ONE

THE DAWN OF A NEW SEASON

A VEIL OF RAIN DESCENDS
watercolour, 11 × 8

During *Bōshu*, rainy days increase. When I was a child, I walked to school every day, past rice paddies newly flooded for planting. I can almost hear the pitter-patter of raindrops starting to fall.

今すぐに、鉛筆と紙を手に
すればいい。それだけだ。

All you need to do is
pick up a pencil and paper
right now. That's all.

TARO OKAMOTO

THE WESTERN CALENDAR has only four seasons; the old Japanese solar calendar—brought to Japan from China 1,200 years ago during Japan's Heian period—has twenty-four. The Japanese, with their deep appreciation for nature, further subdivided the year into seventy-two micro-seasons. For centuries, these micro-seasons were fundamental to Japanese social and artistic expression, especially among the urban aristocracy, and they influenced nearly all major literary and artistic forms and gestures.

Bōshu (early June), the ninth of these twenty-four seasons, is a critical period for farmers, a time when they prepare their fields and sow the seeds that will yield a bountiful harvest. Cumulus clouds billow in the sky, thunder rumbles, and the air crackles with summer's energy. The lush green leaves rustle in the wind, stirring the soul.

Watching my daughter, vibrant with youthful energy, poised to leave the nest, I see a parallel. She, too, is following a natural cycle, a time of sowing seeds for her own future. My role as mother shifts and changes but, like the seasons, it continues. A whirlwind of joy, sorrow, and hope swirls within me. It's time to give voice to these emotions, to plant new seeds of thought in my own heart. What will bloom from these seeds?

FLOWERS OF *BŌSHU*
watercolour,
9 × 12

My late mother's birthday fell during *Bōshu*, the enchanting season when the hydrangeas bloom. They were her most beloved flower.

GRADUATION

It is June 16, 2023. Maya, my father, and I are at a busy crossing in downtown Vancouver, patiently awaiting the light. My eighty-seven-year-old father has come all the way from Japan to attend Maya's graduation, and now he proudly holds two large bouquets of flowers, elegantly wrapped, one for her and one for her boyfriend, Micah, who waits for us at the Orpheum Theatre. My father is dressed impeccably in a light brown fedora, dark brown slacks, and a dress shirt of blue tartan, and he exudes, as always, the timeless charm of a gentleman. Maya's black graduation robe hides her graduation dress, a chiffon creation of light purple and pink that we chose together. I glance over at her. She rarely wears such makeup: bright red lipstick, black mascara, and brown eyeshadow. The makeup accentuates her angelic face and makes her look so grown-up that I almost don't recognize her.

Even with my precarious health, this day feels almost too perfect to be real. My father is beside me after years of estrangement born of the pain of my mother's cancer and the isolating years of the pandemic. My daughter is blossoming into a young woman before my eyes. If only Yoko, my mother, were here. Auspiciously, today is her birthday. She would have been eighty-four today. As the light changes and we cross, our excitement growing, I know somehow that my mother is watching us.

Outside the Orpheum Theatre, hundreds of graduates and their families gather. Everyone is smartly dressed.

They soon transform the usually quiet Vancouver downtown into something more akin to the Shibuya Scramble Crossing in Tokyo, where seas of people surge across streets, creating synchronicity in chaos. Laughter ripples, brightening the atmosphere. Near the entrance, Maya bids us farewell to join her friends in preparation for the ceremony. Maya seems excited, but impatient, too. Then a voice calls out from behind me, "Are you Maya's mom?"

I turn to see a familiar face, but I cannot quite place her. Then I realize she resembles Micah. "Oh, my goodness, are you Micah's sister?" I exclaim. Behind her, standing with an air of quiet elegance, is a striking woman in a vibrant red dress. My eyes widen in excitement. It is Micah's mother! "I've been eager to meet you!" I cry, barely containing my emotions.

Micah's mother, Noa, approaches us with warm smiles and a slight bow. She speaks in Mandarin; Micah's sister, Karmia, interprets: "My mom is delighted to finally meet you. She says she now understands why Maya turned out to be so wonderful—because of you."

I am deeply touched by their kind words. Again, life feels almost too perfect.

My father and I finally make our way inside the Orpheum and locate our seats in the last row, the one reserved for wheelchair users and their companions. My father eagerly searches for Maya's and Micah's names in the program that lists the 400-plus members of the Class of 2023. Meanwhile, I scan the flood of students in their full regalia, caps and tassels bobbing. I realize it is my first experience of a high-school graduation ceremony in North America. It is a first for my father as well, although for him, coming from Japan, everything in Vancouver seems out of the ordinary. Surprisingly, though we are still in the Covid era, no one is wearing a mask. Perhaps they are prioritizing the photographs, photographs that will be cherished forever. Holding my iPhone, I, too, take countless photos, even before the ceremony begins.

The formal ritual is moving, humourous, and entertaining, brimming with hope and love. I observe each student as they confidently take centre stage to receive their certificate. One student does the moonwalk, another, astonishingly, a backflip. Beside me, my father smiles and applauds enthusiastically for each student, as if he knows each one of them.

After three hours, we reach the climax: the announcement of awards. In the program I note the words *The Churchill Scholar Award* just as Maya's name rings out. My mouth falls open; my eyes widen as I try to convey the news to my father.

The announcer continues: "The recipient of the Governor General's Bronze Medal, awarded for academic excellence to the student with the highest graduating average. And also, the 2023 Churchill Scholar Award recipient, Maya Honda-Granirer!" The announcer goes on to say how every one of her teachers was impressed by her exceptional intellect and love of learning, how

Maya brought extraordinary enthusiasm, curiosity, and dedication to all her classes, and how she remained characteristically modest about her achievements.

The crowd erupts into cheers and applause. Maya has achieved the rare distinction of a perfect predicted IB (International Baccalaureate) score of 45. While this is undoubtedly a significant accomplishment, I am most heartened to hear how her teachers commend her modesty. I think how, in an era that often prizes self-promotion and assertiveness, her humility shines as a beacon of grace and genuine character. My cheeks flood with warm tears. I silently thank all the teachers who recognized her talent and brought out the best in her. "You did it, Maya," I whisper. I never had to urge her to study; she was a self-starter from the very beginning, always eager to explore the world around her. Whether on the playground or in preschool, she displayed a remarkable sense of curiosity and a desire to discover things for herself.

My father continues to clap in sheer joy, crying out: "*Sugoi! Sugoi!*" (Amazing! Amazing!). I have never seen him so happy. What a gift to him, I think, for this to happen on his late wife's birthday. What a gift to me. And what a gift to my mother, who is surely watching over the ceremony. Yes, this is my happiest moment.

ABSENCE

Right after Maya's graduation, summer break begins. This is the final opportunity for me to share meaningful moments with Maya before she leaves for university in Toronto, on the opposite side of the continent. I'm also deeply involved in my new summer project, a non-profit documentary film about ground-up social change, which also provides a valuable learning opportunity to three full-time student employees. This leaves me with little free time, but I want to make the best of what time I have. I suggest some joint outings, perhaps to a fancy dinner, perhaps a drive to a nearby beach or shopping mall. Nothing captures Maya's interest. Meanwhile, Maya and Micah express their desire to travel to Japan on what they call a graduation trip—a concept unfamiliar to me. Despite my reservations about the trip and my concerns about their sleeping arrangements, I agree.

I understand that this is our last summer together, and I feel overwhelmed by urgency. I am already experiencing separation anxiety. I often express frustration, asking her, "Can you not schedule something this weekend for us? Something?" Soon, she will be off to Japan.

One day, my friend Debra Sparrow, a Musqueam weaver, comes to bid farewell to Maya. Her black dress is elegantly draped, and a woven blanket in shades of red, black, and mustard rests on her shoulder. She brings a bouquet of red roses for Maya and a pot of mini roses for me. Handing me the pot, she says, "This way, you both will always be connected. Keiko, think of these as symbols of Maya, and take care of your mini roses. They will continue to bloom, just like Maya will in her journey." She removes her woven blanket and places it in Maya's hands, saying, "Take this with you to Toronto. It will keep you warm."

I see Maya's face light up. With tears in my eyes, I thank Debra. Words seem inadequate. Her profound wisdom and her love for Maya opens new perspectives for me. I try to become less centred on "taking" Maya's time for the sake of shared memories and more on appreciating our deep connections.

On that night, I decide to create a message book for Maya to take with her to Toronto. It will be a farewell gift for her new journey. Carrying the blank notebook with me everywhere, I invite my friends to pen messages to remind her of the support they have given us over the years. With a long summer ahead without my daughter, crafting the message book becomes a source of connection and solace. On the blank, cream-coloured cover of the book, I carefully write Maya's name in bold black *kanji*—Japanese characters adapted from Chinese. I then add our family's *kamon*, a traditional Japanese crest unique to our lineage. These crests connect us to our ancestors and often use minimalist geometric shapes and natural, plant-like patterns. Ours is a stylized five-petaled plum blossom. Perhaps Debra's mantra—"Know who you are and know where you came from"—is subconsciously guiding my hand. My gift is nearly complete, imbued with the love of all our friends and the legacy of ancestors.

ROSE MEANS DIFFERENT NOW
watercolour, 9 × 12

The mini roses Debra Sparrow gifted me, symbolic of Maya, grace my kitchen window. As a novice gardener, I find caring for these roses more challenging than raising Maya!

DEPARTURE

On August 29, 2023, I find myself on a journey to Toronto, accompanying Maya as she launches her university adventure. It has been fourteen years since we first arrived in Vancouver from New York, when Maya was just a four-year-old child. And though I have never been to Toronto, returning to the East Coast evokes nostalgic feelings. I gaze out of the porthole window, pressing my face gently against the glass at the world below, but all I can see are thousands of mountain peaks and ridges. The majestic white clouds drift across the vast horizon, and as I watch them, I am filled with wonder at the limitless possibilities that lie ahead for Maya.

It is a red-eye flight, and Maya drifts off to sleep beside me, wrapped snugly in the airline blanket. When is the last time I have seen her sleeping so peacefully so close to me? As she sleeps, the years seem to melt away, and I see the infant she once was. As I gaze at her serene and innocent face, I long to freeze this tender moment. I grab my travel journal and start sketching her sleeping form, trying to capture the charm of her distinctive button nose and long, elegant eyelashes. As I sketch, my love for her surges, a powerful current connecting me to the child she once was, and to the woman she will become. Suddenly, Pumpkin, my faithful feline companion, left at home, crosses my mind. I miss her dearly. Yet, knowing my neighbour is checking on her daily brings a sense of comfort. Somehow, I feel Pumpkin is rooting for me on this important mission.

Glancing at the airplane monitor, I see we still have another three hours to go. I am determined to hit the ground running upon landing in Toronto, and so I opt to grab some rest. I wake to the gentle clinking of dishes and the murmur of voices. The flight attendant is distributing menus and *oshibori*—those wonderfully refreshing, hot, moist towels, a thoughtful touch borrowed from Japanese tradition. Kudos to Air Canada! For breakfast, I choose a cheese omelet and fruit salad; Maya orders the pancakes with fresh cream and berries. Despite the early hour, we are hungry.

My excitement is almost uncontainable. It seems a small miracle to me, being on the plane and travelling with Maya to a city I have never seen before. Even considering the challenges imposed by the not-over-yet Covid pandemic (with recent warnings to brace for another surge this fall and winter), my staycations have been exceptionally prolonged. I have not been on an airplane for seven years. And while for most able-bodied mothers the flight might be as routine as hopping on and off a bus, for me the challenges are many.

After breakfast, I continue to doodle in my journal; but this time, I begin listing ideas for my next project—perhaps a sequel to my debut memoir.

I write at the top of the page: *Developing my Mind by Connecting the Dots.* And then I jot down:

- empty nest
- aging body, 55 years old
- seeking hope
- transitioning from personal to collective success
- what I find inspiring
- the greeting of: "Hello, Toronto!"
- grieving my beloved late uncle, Tetsurō
- new and unknown relationships
- to date or not to date
- generational divides
- silent connections
- the writer as an identity

For a moment, I imagine observing myself from above. Here I sit on a plane bound for an unfamiliar destination, where a too-brief goodbye will mark the beginning of the post-Maya era—now a blank canvas. I am cultivating hope and energy within myself and using my journal as a guide. Perhaps it is my way of grappling with the impending sorrow, or perhaps a way of fending off the waves of change that are sure to come. I recall a Buddhist monk on YouTube saying that we are continuously born and reborn with each passing moment. That, I believe, is the essence of it—life as a constant unfolding, a perpetual cycle of change and renewal. The ever-changing shapes of the clouds outside my porthole seem to mirror my own fleeting thoughts.

I close my journal and stow it, preparing to descend and to immerse myself in Toronto. A sense lingers that I might forge a long-term relationship with this city.

REDISCOVERING MUSEUMS

During the first few days, Maya and I explore the University of Toronto campus and visit various museums, including the Royal Ontario Museum (ROM), the Art Gallery of Ontario (AGO), and the Gardiner Museum. These are located conveniently near our hotel, reminding me of my time in Manhattan where the museums were at my doorstep. Stepping into museums seems so natural, like breathing, effortless and essential. Coming from Vancouver, where museums are scarce, I feel like a fish returning to water.

SHE IS STILL THE SAME
watercolour
11 × 8

No matter how old she becomes, her sleeping face will always remind me of her babyhood. I could gaze at it forever. I remember how, when I was a teenager, my mother said the same thing about me. Only a mother truly understands.

When was the last time I explored a museum with Maya? I wonder. Watching her stride ahead as a grown-up, nostalgia washes over me. Beginning when Maya was three, we would frequent New York's Metropolitan Museum (usually just called the Met) for their free kids' program, which was offered twice a week in the summer. Despite each tour group comprising often more than twenty kids and their adults, the program was impeccably organized. I loved that they were teaching the children both how to engage with art and how to be curious about its creation. I delighted in observing both the artifacts and the children's reactions to the guide's questions. The children were keen observers indeed. I was the only adult companion in a wheelchair and our volunteer guide, Denise, always went above and beyond to assist us, often discretely treating Maya to a small stuffed animal or souvenir from the museum shop.

After each program, we would linger outside the Met on the front steps, Maya playing with Denise and our tour friends, the children jumping and chasing each other in the summer heat. Our adventures always concluded with popsicles. What memories!

OUR FIRST MUSEUM destination is the Art Gallery of Ontario. We begin in the Canadian Art section. I am admiring Tom Thomson's oil paintings (so reminiscent of my home in Vancouver) when I notice that Maya is taking time with each artwork and moving unusually slowly. Surprisingly, she isn't even constantly checking her iPhone as she usually does. Meanwhile, I am eager to see everything before lunch, and so I race ahead. Glancing back, I realize I have left her behind. I turn around and spot her in the Modern Art section. She is standing completely still before David Smith's sculpture, *O Drawing*, her gaze fixed. Between Maya and the sculpture there seems an intense connection, as if they are inhabiting a world within the world. As she moves from work to work, she meticulously reads every description. The next painting, an abstract piece featuring a combination of dark brown, sage, ochre, and bordeaux, keeps her attention for a long time. She is alone with the painting. No wonder I lost her in the gallery.

I finally approach her. "Is it interesting?" I ask.

"Yes, I'm quite drawn to the composition," she replies with poise. I am taken aback, impressed by her mature response. The intellectual resemblance to Dan, my ex-husband, is striking; it is like seeing him reflected in her. We'd explored countless museums around the world together. Like father, like daughter.

"Maya, would you mind if I wait for you at the cafe?" I suggest, pointing to the map I hold in my hand. As I make my way, I take a quick detour through the David Milne collection, the highlight of my visit. I adore his work: watercolour and oil paintings of soft clouds floating in the sky above the plain country fields or lakes. His paintings drive me back to my own watercolour practice, and his writings about seclusion in the wilderness resonate deeply with me, evoking a sense of connection and camaraderie. I think of how I will return to Vancouver alone, and I wonder whether I will find solace in a simple and solitary life as Milne did, focused on writing and painting.

The museum cafe is nestled within the Sculpture Atrium and showcases a captivating hanging sculpture by Haegue Yang titled *Woven Currents—Confluence of Parallels*. As I order my usual Americano and settle in to wait for Maya, I wonder whether her early exposure to the Met during her formative years is responsible for her profound love of art and her ability to engage with it.

I glance at a well-dressed woman sitting alone, engrossed in typing on her laptop, and drift into a daydream. Imagine living near the AGO and visiting it every day! I sip my coffee, relishing the idea of the museum becoming my personal sanctuary. Soon, Maya joins me. We compare notes and study the museum map to plan our next adventure. I glance at her. I almost can't believe this is happening; it is like some surreal but beautiful dream: the museums, Maya, our shared experience. I sense that time is slipping away all too quickly.

In the following days, we visit the ROM and the Gardiner Museum. As she did at the AGO, Maya proceeds slowly, meticulously absorbing each artwork and written description. I find myself watching once again this previously unrevealed aspect of her personality. I adjust my pace to hers, eager to be immersed in her world. Witnessing her curiosity and focus brings me profound joy. I have discovered a new strength within her—a resilience and curiosity capable of conquering any challenge.

Exploring a museum with an art enthusiast is an enriching experience, especially when that person happens to be my beloved daughter. What more could I ask for?

BREAKING AN ISOLATED SYSTEM

"I can't believe it's happening," I whisper. My heart pounds as I watch the light turn yellow on the power gauge of my electric wheelchair. When I left my hotel just moments ago, the gauge had displayed its triumphant trio of three green dots, signaling a fully charged battery. Being confined to a wheelchair is always a daily struggle. "But please not today," I pray.

I have meticulously planned this trip for months, this arduous cross-country journey from Vancouver. It is my last chance to be with Maya—my best friend, my daughter, my life—on this trip, before everything changes in ways neither of us can predict.

With trembling hands, I carefully manoeuvre the joystick, guiding the wheelchair forward ever so slowly. I stop and reset the power button, hoping to squeeze every ounce of energy from the battery. The anticipation is almost unbearable. The yellow light is now down from four to two.

"No way, I hardly moved at all, and yet..." I quickly rush into a nearby cafe so I can charge my chair.

After an hour of charging, I reset the power button again. "What?!" The yellow light remains at two, almost at the red light—at the end of mobility. This should not be happening! Flooded with intense anxiety, I leave the cafe.

The bustling sidewalk stretches ahead, but it is constricted between modern skyscrapers and century-old brownstone heritage buildings. As I observe the carefree passersby, envy mixes with an awareness of my distinctive status. I am a human enveloped by a machine, forming what can be described as an isolated system. In thermodynamics, an isolated system is one with no external energy coming in, and with none leaving. My chair and I epitomize that type of system. I only have a limited amount of energy, preset by the battery. Unlike these nonchalant passersby, who can replenish their energy by eating a snack, I cannot easily obtain the energy I so desperately require.

I have a tough decision to make. Maya has a brief window of time before her semester begins, and my chair's battery is failing. The power gauge continues to taunt me with its unrelenting yellow glow. I am in a race against the fading battery. The thought of returning to the hotel, of giving up my long-awaited excursion with her, cuts me like a dagger. Unable to mask the grief in my voice, I phone and ask a wheelchair Uber to take me back to the hotel. I then search for a rental electric wheelchair, deciding to leave my own chair behind. This invites uncertain and troubling risks, but it is the only way I can ensure I will be able to join my daughter and explore this new city.

The rented chair arrives quickly, and I feel a mix of frustration and determination. This chair has its own problems: it is oversized, its seat cushion is thin, its joystick badly synced, and its speed is 50 percent slower than my own chair. But it has a viable battery. Things are not going as planned, but nothing will stop me from being there for my daughter and for my future self, who desperately needs my present self to succeed.

The road is long. The new chair is so big that my feet dangle in the air every time I travel over a bump and barely touch the footrest when I stop. The thin seat cushion only adds to my discomfort and pain. There are moments of despair and exhaustion, but I am as determined as I have ever been. And we do manage to visit all the places we had jointly planned before our trip, including the campus, the AGO, the ROM, the Gardiner Museum, Chinatown, Kensington and St. Lawrence Markets, some local bookstores, and several well-recommended ethnic restaurants. Every block we traverse increases our shared knowledge of this city and helps us bond with it and with each other, and this keeps pulling me from place to place. Visiting the museums is the most extraordinary part of the trip.

On our last day, we finally visit the Spadina Museum, which sits perched atop a ravine overlooking Toronto. We ascend the steep slope from the last bus stop. The view is unforgettable. The historic mansion tour is captivating. In the adjacent garden, we discover a peaceful spot shaded by large, old trees where the last cicadas of the season fill the warm air with their mating songs. The sweet scent of freshly cut grass evokes vivid memories of my fifteen years living in New York with its hazy east-coast summers. We sit in comfortable silence, but my heart yearns for more conversation as the precious time flies by. Soon, we must head back to our dinner destination.

NOW I HAVE to navigate the descent down the steep slope with the unfamiliar wheelchair, which lacks, I discover, a proper braking system. The path is narrow, and so Maya must walk behind me. After some experimentation, I realize that the only way to apply the brakes is to use both hands to manually pull the right-side hand brake—a manoeuvre utterly impossible while also controlling the joystick with that same right hand. The slope is narrow, and on one side is a steep drop overlooking a high-traffic road. Every time I stop, the chair automatically starts rolling towards the edge, pulled by gravity, forcing me to quickly reverse its trajectory. After a few zigzag trials and occasional skidding, I finally bring the chair to a diagonal stop. I cry out, gripped by a paralyzing terror of tumbling off the cliff and colliding with the traffic below. The last thing I want is to meet an untimely end in a preventable accident just before my daughter's semester begins.

"I can't do this. I'll go off the cliff if I try to move forward again. I don't know what to do!" My voice is so loud and distressed that a passerby on the other side of the street, far away, casts a suspicious glance in our direction.

"Mom, please, calm down. I'm holding onto your chair from behind, and I'll pull to give you counter-tension. Trust me. I've got this."

"Are you sure? Really sure?" My voice trembles with tears. I have never shown this vulnerable and frantic side of myself to my daughter before.

Each step forward on the steep fifty-metre slope is a testament to the trust I place in my daughter. She is infusing her energy into my chair, creating a connection that breaks the isolation of the thermodynamic system. Together, we now form a single, integrated system and descend the hill with unwavering focus and precision.

As I roll along, I find myself recalling many of the moments we have shared throughout the years. From her first steps as a child to her high-school graduation, every milestone has been a shared triumph. I cherish memories of baby Maya sitting on my lap as I manoeuvred my electric chair down busy streets and to the smiles of strangers. Now, as she guides my chair downhill, it strikes me that we have always been sources of support and love for each other. Tears well in my eyes, a mix of residual terror from the steep descent and from overwhelming gratitude for her.

Finally, we reach the bottom of the slope, and I see Maya's familiar face beaming at me with that "See! I told you!" expression. Tears come again as I hug her tightly. My heart still races with adrenalin. She is breathing hard. It is as if we, as one, have just sprinted around a fifty-metre track. In that moment, I know that this trip is worth any terror I might experience.

That evening, as we sit across from each other at a restaurant table, my fear over that yellow light on the wheelchair's power gauge fades from my memory. All I think of now is my daughter's warm embrace and the promise of a new beginning together, even though we will be separated by the vast expanse of the country. It feels, indeed, as if I have had my own matriculation ceremony into a new phase of life.

In that moment, I become belatedly aware of the many invisible transfers of energy that have flowed between other people and my chair-bound self for all these years. We all build these little systems around ourselves. And, from time to time, when life keeps its promises, we have the chance to join our systems with those of others, creating fleeting yet beautiful moments of connection and shared experience. I whisper, "Never forget my *shoshin*," the words famously coined by Zeami. *Shoshin* (初心) is often translated as "beginner's mind," but Zeami believed it meant more than simply being a novice. It meant remembering the lessons learned from overcoming past challenges and approaching each new situation with fresh eyes and an open heart. I will not forget our visit to the Spadina Museum. The summer is already fading faster than I wish.

TWO
WHITE DEW

AWAITING THE WHITE DEW
watercolour, 4 × 6

September, and the echinacea still thrives in my front yard, a vibrant splash of pink until the first frost claims its beauty.

秋風は吹きむすべども白露の
みだれて置かぬ草の葉ぞなき

The autumn wind, wild and free,
scatters the dew on every leaf.

DAINI NO SANMI

EVEN THOUGH summer's heat still lingers, I can sense the subtle arrival of autumn. The season of White Dew has begun, marked by cool mornings and evenings. White Dew. What an evocative term! It speaks to the profound connection ancient Japanese people had with the natural world, their ability to find poetry in the simple act of observing the tiny, glistening dewdrops adorning plants at dawn and dusk, a sensibility that seems sadly lost in our modern world.

The *Hyakunin Isshu* is a collection of poetry featuring one poem from each of a hundred renowned poets spanning the Asuka to Kamakura periods. The *Hyakunin Isshu* transcends mere literature; it embodies the very soul of Japanese culture and has been cherished for centuries both as a collection of exquisite poems and as a beloved card game. In high school, I was a member of the *Hyakunin Isshu* club, and I still have a deep appreciation for the enduring beauty of this collection.

Like the poet Daini no Sanmi, daughter of the brilliant Murasaki Shikibu, author of *The Tale of Genji* I am deeply moved by the autumn wind stirring the dew-laden leaves. A sense of profound connection to this poet from over a millennium ago washes over me. This gentle movement mirrors the emotions stirring within, a poignant reminder of the bittersweet beauty of this time of year. I take a deep breath, gazing out the window at the maple leaves shimmering with dew, finding solace in their quiet elegance.

HOMECOMING

After struggling, once again, with the near-dead battery in my motorized travel wheelchair, I finally arrive home from Toronto. The cooler September air is so refreshing compared to the Toronto heat. How I missed the fresh air filled with the scent of trees! After rolling through the door, I am comforted by moving into my still-functional at-home wheelchair. I head for bed for a badly needed sleep. But when I get into my personal elevator to go upstairs to the bedroom, I discover it is broken. First the chair, then the elevator! Is the household deity that protects my machines failing me?

I remain at home for the whole week to recuperate and have the elevator fixed. It is a far from mundane week. A handful of friends visit at various times. At first they come for urgent check-ups and to assist with transforming my downstairs couch so that I have a place to sleep until the elevator is fixed. Others come to join me for morning coffee. Each day is marked by unique moments, almost as though I have orchestrated a meticulously planned series of homecoming events.

I maintain a connection with Maya through small gestures, such as sending her brief, cheerful texts and sharing photos. These include shots of our cat, Pumpkin, and of me wearing my newly acquired hoodie with a University of Toronto logo. Her sporadic responses cause my heart to brim with gratitude, but occasionally I wonder if I am reaching out too often.

The unexpected elevator malfunction forces me to adapt to new routines, such as sleeping downstairs. I remain acutely attuned to my immediate surroundings; I do not want further complications, and so I am cautious and diligent. My reflections start shifting away from my recently emptied nest towards the present and towards appreciating the deep support offered by friends. Surprisingly, I do not feel alone.

Following my indoor week, I feel compelled to step outside for various errands, one of which is to visit a nearby bank. The early September afternoon is bathed in warm sunlight, and I decide to make the journey using my electric wheelchair—thankfully fully functional—and a public bus. The bus driver greets me with a smile and patiently waits for me to secure my chair in place. This courtesy is in notable contrast to Toronto, where none of the bus drivers would pause to allow me to get properly situated.

As I ride the bus and watch the familiar sights pass by the window, a lump forms in my throat, and an inner voice stirs, reminding me with a poignant twinge, *She is gone from here.* The tree-lined sidewalks that Maya and I traversed together for the better part of fifteen years appear strangely devoid of their former vitality and energy. I know she is not here in this city, but still my eyes fill with tears as they search for her likeness. In the distance, I spy a group of high schoolers congregating at a bus stop, playfully engaging with one another. I shake my head and embrace a new thought: She is on a path of her own because I have raised her well. It is a way of finding solace.

My familiar neighbourhood displays unexpected kindness all that day. A random passerby kindly presses the traffic light button for me and continues on their way. A middle-aged man wearing a turban graciously holds the bank door for me. Even the busy bakery cashier steps out of her booth to assist my exit. As I pass by, people on the street offer warm smiles and nods of acknowledgement. The air is filled with the sweet, familiar scent of trees, and everything seems to radiate . . . euphoria.

Before long, I find myself smiling and breathing deeply, appreciating the late afternoon's golden air. I've often heard others say that Vancouver may be less rich in art and culture than some other cities, but that it is a pleasant place to return to after travelling. "This is my home," I whisper, as if reaffirming my connection. In that moment, all my anxieties about Maya's departure and the looming empty nest simply recede, replaced by a sense of peace.

On my trip home, I observe the commuting students on the bus and feel as connected to them as if they were my own children, a sensation I never experienced when my daughter was with me. In the past, there has always been a distinction between "mine" and "theirs." Now they all deserve my full support. I find myself seeing all children and youth as precious.

"Will you come back to Vancouver during the winter break?" I ask her over FaceTime. It is still late September, yet I can hardly contain my longing to see her again.

"Maybe," Maya replies without any expression on her face.

"What do you mean, 'maybe'?" I reply with mounting anxiety.

After an awkward pause, she says in a firm, detached voice, "Umm, I'll be back in Vancouver, but I'm not coming back to *your* place."

Thunderstruck, I blurt out, "What?! Why?! Where would you stay, then?" I am trembling.

"I don't know yet. I'll still come see you," she calmly replies.

"Why? Why can't you stay at *our* home?" I am so anxious that I cannot tell if I am begging or threatening.

"Umm, because I can't see my friends freely whenever I want to if I'm with you. And you knew this already. I'll never come back to your home from now on. I made up my mind way before I left for Toronto."

"No, I did not know that! I've raised you with my best intentions, though I'm not perfect. And you know how much I want to see you. I've been looking forward to spending some mother–daughter time ever since you left Vancouver. Your boyfriend is welcome to sleep over in our house, too. Why can't you stay over even one night?" I feel a great pain inside and can hardly breathe. I am on the verge of crying.

ON HER NINETEENTH BIRTHDAY
watercolour, 4 × 6

For her nineteenth birthday, I paint her portrait, trying to capture the essence of the child I knew: those curious, sparkling eyes that still hold a hint of the toddler she once was. But the truth is, she is now a beautiful adult woman, filling me with immense pride and gratitude.

“Umm, because you’re overbearing. And I already decided, and I don’t want to talk about it now,” she says without emotion.

“Please reconsider, Maya . . . please.”

After that conversation, I feel surges of anger, and then disappointment in both in her and myself. And then I gradually descend into a profound abyss, contemplating this abrupt and unexpected reality, a reality that I could never have imagined just ten minutes ago. Oh, the double blow of loneliness and cold rejection! Have I done something wrong? I raised a kind daughter who should honour and respect her mother. Why has she suddenly become so distant? Have I unintentionally hindered her freedom in my parenting? Is there some defining moment, or . . . ? What did she mean when she said “I should have known”?

Yes, I know I am overbearing in certain areas, such as expecting her to contribute to household chores and to navigate dating responsibly. How do other mothers maintain a close relationship with their teenage daughters without provoking feelings of being stifled? What if she believes that I don’t love her? A wave of regret washes over me. I wish I had listened to her more, been more tender.

Being unable to reach out to my ex-husband to share my bruised heart makes me feel even lonelier. Out of desperation, I text my sister in Japan. “Sister, it feels like she cut the bond with me, and I have nothing but the ‘why.’ Should I imagine that I don’t have a daughter?”

She texts back, “No worries at all. All you can do is wait. As she may be struggling to adjust in a new environment we just need to watch over quietly without interfering." Then she adds, "Keiko, you are her mother! Do your best!"

I am her mother indeed. My mother used to say, especially during my most rebellious phase in my early twenties, "I will never give up, because you are my daughter. No matter how far away you are from me around the globe, I will always be ready to support you and work hard." I remember my ambivalence, how I felt exasperated every time my mom shared her emotions but how, at the same time, I felt, deep inside, secure and loved by her words. Could I explain all this to my daughter now?

Did my mom ever doubt my love for her or lose confidence in our bond? I wonder. Even if she didn't, I was quite harsh towards her at times, speaking sharply, maintaining only sporadic contact in my late teens and early twenties. I had no clue who I was back then. And my mother *was* over-protective and overbearing, forcing a rupture. Suddenly I see Maya in my younger self, or vice versa.

Her words, "I will not be coming back to your place," keep echoing in my head and battering my heart. But this time, they sound different. Trying to get a grip on my emotions, I focus on the unvoiced meaning beneath the surface. Although I still do not fully understand, I keep my eyes closed and listen to the silent, empty nest. Our bond is still intact. I embrace her independence. Her warning is her declaration of her own independence and an unsought invitation for me to find my own.

The next morning, I send her a photo of my recent watercolour painting along with a text: "Hi, Maya, after some reflection, I will respect your decision, as my intention is to give you as much space and independence as you want. I sincerely hope that you will let me know what you need to repair our relationship. I want to have a good relationship with my daughter as I move forward and don't want to have this feeling of rejection and alienation. Just to let you know, I do support your relationship with your boyfriend. I love you, Maya."

On National Daughters Day, we exchange two heart emojis in a text. Though a sense of unease lingers, I look beyond it, picturing the sun, its enduring light. My love for Maya is like that—steadfast, unwavering, present even in the deepest darkness. Quietly, I whisper: "We'll be okay, no matter what."

MEETING MY YOUNGER SELF

I left Japan at age 26 to get married. My late mother remarked, "You've run to the opposite side of the globe to be far away from me." While she was genuinely happy about my choice, she was heartbroken that her cherished daughter, who resembled her so much, flew so far away, never to return. She hoped I would live nearby as an adult one day. Often, in front of my older sister, she'd tell me, "You're just like me." I felt both awkward and honoured by this praise, this apparent favouritism. That is, until my late teens when, much like Maya, I began to rebel against expectations.

MEETING MY YOUNGER SELF
watercolour, 11 × 8

I would tell her, "Follow your heart, not prestige nor others' expectations." I also would add, "But, you did your best, and that is what matters!"

My mother's words haunted me for years, their sting lingering in my heart. Perhaps it's because they hold a kernel of truth, though I couldn't grasp it at the time. Now, in hindsight, everything is clear. "I needed to go to the opposite side of the globe to break free from my dependence on you, because I relied on you too much." I can barely articulate these words, but they echo loudly in my mind. "I'm truly sorry, Mom. I wish I could be closer to you," I whisper, feeling so deeply her pain and longing. Tears well up as memories flood back of missed opportunities to express my love and care for her during my early twenties, back when I lived alone in Tokyo. I was distant and prickly with her for no good reason. Yet, despite my coldness, she showered me with unconditional love and care. Why was I like that? I keep asking this as my own daughter is seeming to mirror my younger self.

After high school, following a disappointing score on a national test, I opted to pursue a career in nursing rather than become a medical doctor, which had been my first choice. I harboured feelings of dissatisfaction with myself. Despite dedicating myself to four years of study, my discontent—or perhaps my insecurity—persisted deep down, even after starting a career as an occupational health nurse at Nippon Telephone and Telegraph, one of the most coveted employers among college graduates.

In my youth, I sought to identify myself with external factors without examining my inner self. I recall one of my nursing professors praising a book she was reading about self-discovery. At the time, lacking any interest in exploring my own identity, I dismissed her remarks as part of a mid-life crisis. Instead, I chased superficial validation—social status, fine clothing, attractive partners and friends, and the illusory connections of social networking. Despite having read numerous philosophical books in my youth, I lived mindlessly, not mindfully. I was also oblivious to the wisdom of my grandparents, parents, and the elders in my hometown. The famous phrase, "Youth is wasted on the young," perfectly described my early twenties. Why couldn't I absorb the wisdom that had surrounded me

"I'M SORRY" ARRANGEMENT
watercolour,
12 × 9

I sometimes compose my mental *ikebana* on paper. I arrange thoughts as flowers. A visual meditation. Lines and shapes become stillness. It's a moment of peace, captured.

since birth? Was I driven by the normal hormonal surges? Was this typical of that era, the early '90s Tokyo? I was a quintessential spoiled child, a part of what in Japan is called the Bubble Generation—a generation that benefited from a period of economic prosperity—and this may have contributed to a sense of entitlement or a lack of understanding about the challenges others faced.

Maybe Maya is charting the same course of transformation that once defined my own journey, battling the unseen tides within. As for my mother, she lost her dream of living near her daughter, of having her forever close by. I wonder: how did she reconcile herself with this loss? Now that I am in her position, I am flooded with guilt and longing and a deep-seated desire to reconcile with Maya. But is it possible? I ponder.

APPLIED LEARNING

I'm getting ready to teach Social Artistry at SFU 55+ for the fourth time, and this makes me think back on how far I've come. The previous term had been a turning point for me; I had poured all my energy and passion into the sessions and had finally begun to understand what applied learning is all about. Now, while reviewing and updating the teaching materials, I constantly consider the student's perspectives. My own evolving inquiries, often quite personal, and my broadening interests encourage me to explore the subject matter more comprehensively.

At age fifty-five, I ponder the implications of this 55+ stage of life: not young anymore, but flexible and resourceful enough to have social agency. While age-related issues are real, age is never the only thing in the room. There is much intersectionality, including all the other identities and personal qualities we bring into our world. As such, in a time of diversity, equity, and inclusion, we are now being challenged more than ever to live authentically and to embrace the uniqueness of others. But there are times when I wonder how I can display my authenticity, especially when it feels uncertain. Other questions I ask: "How can I embrace the authenticity of others?" And: "What kind of society would arise if individuals could leverage their uniqueness together?"

These questions—about difference, acceptance, and imperfection—drive me to teach this course at SFU's 55+ program, even though I do not have answers.

Differences between people can create anxiety and confusion. They also sometimes cause us to turn away from each other. We often find ourselves using black-and-white thinking when we encounter differences. We say that self-acceptance is the foundation for accepting others, yet I wrestle with accepting my own failures and imperfections.

Recently, I had a challenging conversation with my eighty-seven-year-old father regarding inheritance—an unresolved issue looming over my close-knit family, comprising my father, sister, and myself. Despite our closeness, independence, and deep care for each other, there is a lingering disagreement: the inheritance of our family home and land. My father wishes to transfer the property title to my sister, foreseeing that she will likely become his caregiver in his final days. He proposed to offer money and stock to me instead, aiming for fairness. In the heat of an argument, he added, "You left Japan by choice. Your inheritance is my decision. You're thriving in Canada professionally and socially. Why this sudden interest in returning to Japan, given your challenging health status? Here, the city is not wheelchair-friendly. And I cannot live with you anyway." His words cut deep. In his eyes, I am disabled and a burden.

Our online conversation spiraled into chaos, voices overlapping as we struggled to grasp each other's perspectives. My sister attempted to listen, but the mood remained taut. I tried to explain the depth of my emotions: "You don't understand. Our family home in Japan holds profound meaning for me. It's my only stable sanctuary and a vital part of my identity. Why define me solely by my ability to be a caregiver to you?" I cried, grappling with my sudden, fiery temperament.

Then, he attacked again: "All I hear from you is a theory, a mental concept. You don't lose your sense of belonging, even if you don't own the land. And if you interfere with my happiness—my plans to dismantle my old house and build my new, modern, upgraded home—I'll decide. Legally, you're entitled to one eighth of the land. I'll partition that off and rebuild a new house for myself."

His words appalled me; it is the first time I'd heard such harshness from him. Where did his cruelty come from? Money and housing were never issues within our family.

"Our house is fine. Why destroy it? Can't my sister and I decide what to do with the house and land after you're gone?" I asked. I refused to sever my tangible connection to Japan, even though I had no intention of returning there to live. "Why not consider other options?" I continued. "Even if the town isn't wheelchair-accessible or -friendly, I'll ensure it becomes so!" I almost blurted out that I was talking about *him*, not the town. I seethed with anger at the patriarchal system, at his utter lack of compassion or... vision. It became about dignity. I felt a visceral connection to my childhood home and the land, a sense that I was fighting for my very right to exist; though, to be honest, the precise nature of that fight remained unclear.

The conversation ended in bitterness. Unresolved. I vowed not to speak to him any time soon. Then, my sister texted me, "Keiko-chan, I'm sorry I couldn't engage much during the conversation, I was in an online office meeting. Wishing you a nice day." Her message was kind and familiar. She was raised as the responsible elder daughter and peacemaker in our family.

I started to explore why I couldn't let go of my birthright. Why couldn't my father and I escape from black-and-white thinking? Why was I so attached to the small piece of land that I had not visited for nearly two decades? What happens now with our relationship? All I felt capable of at that moment was avoidance. What if I chose to hold firm? Or what if I reconsidered? Could I adopt the notion that belonging is a sentiment, one not solely anchored to the land? What was it I feared so deeply?

These thoughts bring me back to my preparations for teaching my course: Social Artistry Through Co-Creation. In studying co-creation, some key questions inevitably arise: How can we nurture recognition of individual creativity while still fostering collective synergy and avoiding harmful dynamics? How can we create a space that encourages both freedom of expression and respectful dialogue, nurturing trust and unity among participants? These questions deal with issues such as the pressure to conform, the erosion of personal agency, and the emergence of cynicism, withdrawal, and confusion. They are more challenging if our experience of co-creation is limited.

That summer, my team and I embarked on a quest to find visual metaphors for co-creation, a concept that is essential for fostering collective creativity, but that is difficult to define. Among our explorations, we stumbled upon the concept of dynamic range in photography, or the greyscale. Greyscale is a spectrum of shades seamlessly transitioning from pure white to deep black and encompassing the full range of tones in between. Imagine a landscape with a bright sky and deep shadows. A camera with a high dynamic range can capture the details in both the highlights and the shadows, preserving information in both the brightest and darkest areas of the scene. However, a camera with a limited dynamic range struggles to capture this breadth of light and shadow, resulting in an image that is lacking in depth and nuance and that fails to capture the true essence of the scene.

We began to apply this concept to human behaviour and societal dynamics. Just as a camera with limited dynamic range struggles to capture the full spectrum of light, societies that suppress or marginalize certain voices or perspectives fail to achieve their full potential and are trapped in a binary black-and-white mindset. Co-creation, we realized, is about embracing the full spectrum of human experience—the diverse voices, perspectives, and lived experiences that make up our society. It's about creating spaces where all voices are heard, where all perspectives are valued, and where the full range of human potential can be realized. In essence, it's about dissolving boundaries.

I ponder: what if my father and I could metaphorically employ that greyscale to perceive each other's viewpoints and true selves? How would this work in the practical ebb and flow of communication? Given his age, I sense we are in a race against time, leaving me feeling cornered; I am potentially losing either my physical home or my emotional one. I cannot see any grey. Only the black. Only the white.

LOST AND FOUND

In a message to my sister, I pour out my frustration: "I had an online conversation with Maya last night, and it left me feeling more discouraged than ever. Her aloofness is so pronounced. Her silence, combined with a complete lack of facial expression, feels critical, like I'm constantly being judged. I'm starting to wonder if I'm still doing something wrong, if I've somehow failed her. She's become a completely different person. Or... not the same person

ALL THE WORLD'S A STAGE
watercolour, 12 × 9

I sit alone in the neighbourhood cafe watching a young couple or a family, their joy a poignant reminder of my own life that was. Now, I find solace in the pages of a book or the distractions offered by my phone.

anymore." I added, trying to sound more positive, "But I realize that dwelling on this is taking a toll, so I'm trying to put it aside. Tomorrow is my book launch, a momentous occasion, and I need to focus on making it memorable. I'm looking forward to celebrating and creating lasting memories."

She replies, "Life has its ups and downs. I'm sure Maya is doing her best and may be struggling to be honest with her mother. You both feel love. Good luck with your book launch. Just relax and be yourself!"

My sister is always kind and accepting, always offering me reassurance and hope. Her words give me solace; but as soon as we stop texting, I am engulfed in sorrow and loss.

After sunset, the house falls into deep silence. It is dinnertime, but I find myself wandering upstairs, drawn to Maya's bedroom. Some parents I know have already repurposed their off-to-college children's rooms, but I can't bear to change a thing. I leave it as a kind of personal anthropology museum. To enter her room is to enter the realm of her imagination, and it brings me a sense of calm and tenderness. As I stand in front of the large whiteboard where she used to neatly chart ambitious goals and dreams, I slowly begin to reconnect with who my daughter is. All her aspirations have materialized, including her dream of attending a prestigious university.

My eyes drift to the top corner of the whiteboard, where she has written, *I am grateful for... 1) my tidiness, 2) my grandma, 3) my house, 2/14/2016.*

In that year, she would have been just eleven years old. Those simple expressions of gratitude, preserved in faded marker, speak volumes. Her word *tidiness* hints at a self-disciplined nature, a desire for order in her young world. *My grandma*, of course, is my mother, the anchor of our family despite physical distance. And *my house*—that safe, warm haven where she feels secure and loved. It struck me back then, as it does now, that even at that tender age, she possessed a deep appreciation for the constants in her life, the things that truly mattered. I believe she has always had a quiet strength, a gentle spirit, and a profound capacity for love. Even then, her heart was open, her eyes were seeing the good in her world, and she was, in her own way, giving thanks. It makes me wonder what other treasures are hidden on this whiteboard, what other glimpses into her young heart are waiting to be rediscovered. Perhaps, later, I'll take a closer look. I then make my way to her study, once my office but now hers for the past three years. I can now reclaim it, but I have no desire to change this space. Over the last few years, she has spent more time in this room than anywhere else in the house. Her presence is nearly palpable here.

On her long desk, I spot a paperback book embellished with an array of colourful sticky notes. It is *Perfume*, by Patrick Süskind, a novel she pored over for school. The book is filled with these meticulously placed sticky notes, resembling a captivating contemporary work of art. As I examine it, I can vividly envision her painstaking and joyful process of reading. Flipping through the pages, I exclaim, "Wow!" Her detailed, handwritten notes fill every available space on every page and in every variety of colour. The notes are embellished with intricate shapes such as arrows, animated facial expressions, and question marks enclosed in brackets. She used a thin ink pen, and her meticulous handwriting is as readable as printed text. She clearly engaged deeply with the text. At that moment,

I feel I have rediscovered her in the pages, and I briefly forget my anguish and devastation from half an hour ago.

I place the book on my lap and quickly go downstairs to the living room, eager to read the novel. It marks my first time reading a novel that she studied for high school, as well as the first time I have experienced reading a parallel story crafted by my daughter. *What a literary genius*, I think. As I open up to Chapter One, I stumble upon the legend she created to explain the intriguing shapes and colourful codes scattered throughout:

Green = thoughts, observations, key ideas

Blue = influence of our upbringing + ↺ (in blue) + blue sticky note

Red = class/power/wealth + pink sticky note

Orange = the effect of scent + ⇉ (in orange) + orange sticky note

Pale Green = unknown words

Dark Green = questionable sections

Sticky note = key event

Reading the novel becomes an urgent and essential task, a means to reconnect with my daughter. I ask for her permission, which she graciously grants. I approach it slowly, carefully noting all the editorial comments. Surprisingly, this proves to be stimulating and enjoyable, better than any book club experience I had ever had. Alongside creative facial emojis, Maya has included a glossary for difficult words as well as a plethora of irresistible and highly entertaining expressions, such as: *WTF, LOL, Creepy, I disagree, I want this perfume, Very true, Noooo.* And much more. I find myself chuckling often, as though I am back in high school working with a brilliant study partner. Literature is not my strong suit, but Maya's guidance in understanding the text is skillful and entertaining.

Perfume transports me to eighteenth-century France, where I follow the chilling journey of Jean-Baptiste Grenouille, a man with an uncanny sense of smell. The novel vividly depicts a world of scent, both sublime and horrifying, a descent into darkness that captivates and repels me in equal measure. I wonder what Maya, with her own unique perspective, made of this dark and mesmerizing tale.

Over the following week, I immerse myself further in Patrick Süskind's novel and in the imaginative, insightful mind of my daughter. Despair at my empty nest and illusion of disconnection never once crosses my mind. Instead, I am enveloped by feelings of connection and understanding. It is a revelation, reaffirming the transformative power of storytelling to bridge gaps and forge bonds.

The sound of Maya's footsteps whispers through the hallways. They echo in my mind. I read her witty notes about the novel *Perfume* and then study the infrequent heart emojis she has sent by text. These small, everyday moments, often overlooked in the rush of life, unexpectedly become my White Dew season, a newfound beauty amid the changing seasons of life.

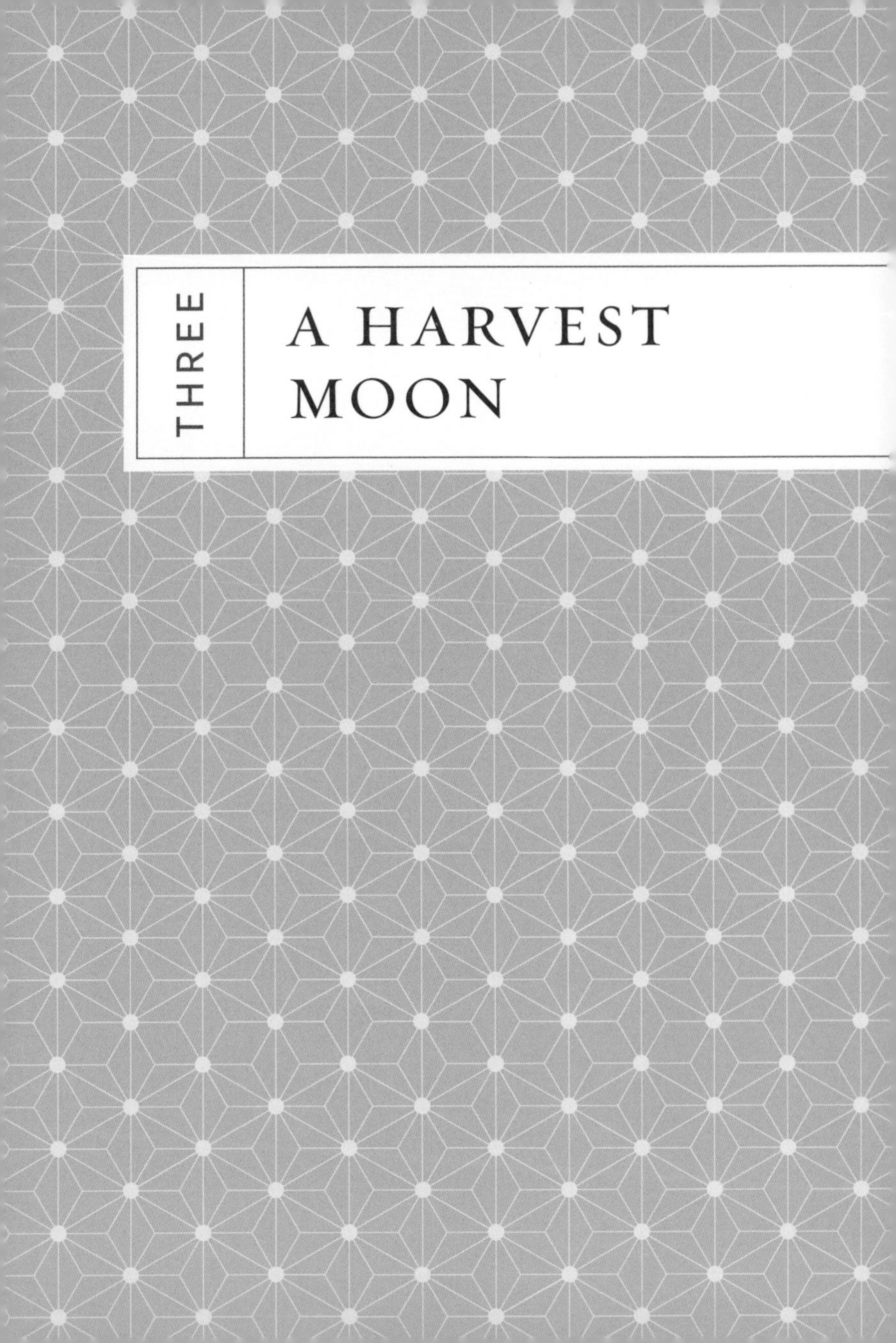

THREE
A HARVEST MOON

DREAMS IN THE EMPTY NEST
watercolour, 9 × 12

How does she spend the long autumn nights amid the empty nest? What thoughts occupy her mind beneath the watchful gaze of the stars? What seeds of hope does she nurture within this sanctuary now? Tell me.

女郎花 秋の野風に うちなびき
心ひとつを たれによすらむ

Ominaeshi *swaying in the*
autumn breeze, to whom does
it direct its solitary heart?

FUJIWARA NO TOKIHIRA

IN THE HEART of autumn, the Harvest Moon shines its brightest. It illuminates the night sky like a spotlight, casting its gentle, powerful glow upon us. As the long night deepens, a longing for someone creeps into my heart, carried by the autumn breeze. Even the flowers in my garden sway softly under the moonlight.

I find myself drawn back to the world of classical Japanese poetry, particularly the *Kokin Wakashū*, an early anthology of *waka* (poetry) dating from the Heian period. This collection, with its layers of meaning and sentiment, often explores human eros and the primal instinct of life and sexuality through the playful and ambiguous language of poetry.

One example is a poem by Fujiwara no Tokihira, in which a woman with multiple suitors is compared to a swaying damsel plant. This delicate flower, often associated with feminine grace due to the character 女 (woman) in its name, is itself a metaphor for the woman's perceived fickleness. Written from a man's perspective, the poem leaves the reader pondering his true intentions. Is he genuinely curious about which man has captured her affections? Or does this image of the swaying damsel plant reflect his weariness with her apparent indecisiveness?

The question lingers: Should she choose him? Or perhaps not choose anyone at all? I, for one, find the damsel plant, called *ominaeshi* in Japanese, a most enchanting flower. It blooms with a gentle yet dignified grace, as if to honour the beauty and independence of women.

UNEXPECTED DANCE

"One day, we will dance!" Shu (not his real name) gently extends his hand, as though selecting me as his partner on an imaginary dance floor. His gentle hand and my clumsy hand join like magnets. I can't quite comprehend what is happening. I feel as though I have touched something beautiful but elusive, like hope—but hope for what?

We are clearing the dishes after the film screening salon I hosted that night, and he is one of the guests. I met him once before, four months ago, at a family dinner organized by my trusted male friend who was visiting from afar. Shu is his best friend. Shu is charming, tall, slender, French-speaking, a great conversationalist, and always smiling. Still, the impression, though positive, hasn't lingered. I haven't thought of him since.

In the kitchen, Shu talks passionately about his favourite subjects: wind energy (of which he is an expert), longevity, epigenetics, Dr. David Sinclair's experiments in reversing the biological clock in mice, and his nutritious regimens. He says confidently, "I believe your spinal damage will be completely fixed."

I smile in response, appreciating his genuine conviction and kindness. Yet, I feel a tiny bit of sadness and a sense of distance. I want to say, "My health is fragile, and I should focus on today, not longevity." But I do not.

Soon he is the only guest left. We keep talking until past midnight, discussing our life journeys, our exes, our children, and how to find a work–life balance after turning fifty. Finally, after saying goodbye after midnight, I pinch myself and think, *How did I come to know this energetic and eclectic human being?* I sense we will meet again.

The next day, I share a selfie of Shu and me with my friend, along with a quick recap of the previous night. His text response has a touch of humour, "Did Shu assist you in cleaning up in the kitchen beyond just attending the screening?"

Did my friend give him any instructions on how to be helpful to me? I chuckle and realize I appreciate his concern. "Absolutely," I text back. "Shu is not only helpful but also very attentive. He even spotted a typo in my film, the one I produced and directed!"

"Yes, I'm well aware of his keen attention to detail," my friend replies.

Shu and I start texting the next day. From him: "It was great talking with you last night. Too bad I had to leave! I can't remember what we settled on last night, but getting together on Thursday evening would work for me. You?"

He is leading our dance, and I willingly follow. We agree that I would order sushi from my favourite restaurant and that he would prepare a chocolate fondue for dessert. *How French!* I think, tingling with excitement.

Thursday finally arrives. Aware of Shu's meticulous nature, I take extra care with my appearance, wanting to both look and feel naturally my best. A mix of anticipation and nervousness swirls within me. Is this just dinner between friends? Or something more? We are single adults, free to make our own choices. Despite the uncertainty, I feel surprisingly at ease. His close friendship with someone I trust implicitly is a comforting anchor.

We chat non-stop during the sushi dinner that is complemented perfectly by the Japanese sake he has brought. When dessert time arrives, he moves to the kitchen. From his backpack, he pulls out an assortment of fruits, orange liqueur, whiskey, heavy cream, and two bars of Toblerone Milk Chocolate. With a playful grin, he remarks, "Toblerone chocolate has nougat, perfect for fondue!" After melting the chocolate in a small pan and adding grated orange zest, he licks the melted chocolate from the spatula, nods in approval, and then offers the spatula to me. I follow suit. This indirect kiss tastes sweet and tingling. His hands work with precision, artfully arranging the sliced fruits on two plates. Before long, the plates are adorned with slices of banana, strawberry, orange, peach, raspberry, and kiwi. He then asks if I have any candles. After lighting two candles and dimming the room's lights, our perfect dessert continues until midnight. We share stories from childhood, recount our adventures, and explore his fascinating hobby of flying gliders. I can't help but admire his childlike passion for learning. It is clear to me why he became an engineer.

"Well, it appears it's becoming our tradition," he remarks, glancing at his watch. It reads 12:30 AM, the same time our last encounter ended. As we make our way toward the entrance, he turns to me and asks, "Do you have a guest room? Can I stay overnight?"

I am taken aback by his unexpected suggestion but hear myself replying, "Umm... Yes," surprising myself. It is only our second meeting, yet I feel as though I am caught in an updraft, swept up by some inexplicable force. He gently places his hands on my back and begins to give me a soothing shiatsu massage, carefully pressing the acupressure points. "It's good for your body *and* for your mind. Would you like a full-body massage?" he asks with a hint of playfulness.

"Perhaps next time," I politely reply, feeling shy.

I gently make it clear that I want to sleep alone in my own bedroom, which is located some distance from the guest room. My voice is a little unsteady as I anticipate the potentially awkward conversation about this new, uncharted territory. Thankfully, it doesn't come up. When the time comes to say goodnight, we exchange a goodbye kiss on both cheeks. But then he leans in and gently kisses my lips. It feels so natural and right. A new dance, a dance of connection.

CARPE DIEM

I find myself frequently checking my phone, especially WhatsApp, where I communicate with Shu, my new buddy. Still, I make an effort to keep my expectations at bay. The morning after his first sleepover, he messages me, "I don't know if it was the strong coffee or what, but I felt super giddy the whole drive back to the office!" That text brings a smile to my face.

We exchange more texts and decide to meet again to watch the film *Dumb Money* at a local theatre. In his text,

"*KIYOKU, TADASHIKU, UTSUKUSHIKU*" (BE PURE, PROPER, AND PRETTY)
watercolour, 8 × 13

I remember this phrase from a famous Japanese pop song of the '80s. It seems every teenager in Japan has heard the song at least once. It urges young women to be pure, proper, and pretty, though whether it is encouraging or cynical, I can't recall. I wonder if this idealized image has subconsciously influenced my own self-expectations and perhaps even limited my sense of self.

he affectionately refers to me as "cutie." I smile, unsure how to respond and how to express my warmth without revealing too much too soon. Should I play it sweet? Something more? I hesitate, caught in a moment of awkward charm, wishing I had a readily available arsenal of emojis to respond to his nickname for me.

On our third meeting, he picks me up and drives us in my wheelchair-accessible van to the theatre. The whole thing strangely feels like a blind date—a new and different experience. Even though my van can be a bit temperamental, he handles it with such care that everything goes smoothly. The feeling of comfort, safety, and togetherness is reminiscent of past relationships. However, I feel an imbalance creeping in. I find myself worrying about becoming emotionally dependent—a vulnerability I don't want, a prospect that frightens me. I'm sure many independent women can relate. Nevertheless, I continue to enjoy our time. Before the film starts, we order wine and cheese at the bar. Shu briefs me on the film, sharing his own stock market mishaps. The film, a 2023 biographical comedy-drama, tells the story of the GameStop short squeeze and how ordinary people on Reddit took on Wall Street in 2021. I confess I'm not well versed in these financial topics, but I'm hoping to follow along. It makes me realize how much I still don't know—about the world, and about him.

On our trip back to my place after the screening, I contemplate whether he will simply drop me off or ask to stay overnight again. He mentions that he has to wake up at 4:45 in the morning to take his son to hockey practice, and so it seems likely he will head home that night. The drive also highlights the geographical distance between my house and the centre of things. In that moment, I begin to question my decision to reside at my current house, post-empty nest, especially considering I cannot drive. What am I truly afraid of? Why am I so hesitant to learn to drive and achieve real independence? The realization hits me: I need to be able to drive myself. A truly independent relationship means not relying on one person. Despite my established independence and resources, a wave of self-doubt washes over me. I am taken aback by this sudden shift in my mood.

"I can stay longer, or even spend the night, if you'd like," he mentions as he walks through the door, returning the car key to me.

"Oh, of course, please come in; I'll make some tea," I reply. I wish I could muster more enthusiasm. I am feeling a bit down. Earlier that day, just before he picked me up, I had a phone call with my daughter. Although it isn't something to burden a lovely night with, I can't help but share a bit about the mother–daughter tension that has arisen and my resulting sorrow. He sips his tea and kindly offers a more positive perspective.

Our conversation explores deeper territory as the night progresses. "I could stay the night here, and we could even share the bed," he suggests.

I hesitate, feeling bashful about the idea, not because of him, but because of my... let us say, condition. "I wish

I could be more adventurous, but it feels too fast," I admit. "I'd like us to be friends first, and then I think I'd feel more relaxed about it. Sorry, I don't mean to..." My words trail off without a clear conclusion.

In response, he offers some wisdom: "Listen to your gut and don't overthink it. Follow your intuition."

I open up to him: "I know. I'm already afraid of... of getting my heart broken or losing you as friend. It's funny. I'm already thinking about that."

"*Carpe diem,*" he replies with conviction. "If you don't take risks, you might miss out on life."

After contemplating this, I say, "Okay, let's give it a try. But I can only lie down next to you for about an hour or so."

He grins warmly and gently pushes my wheelchair. "That's fine. I'm safe!" he reassures me.

He dims the lights of my guest room until we can barely see each other's faces, but soon my eyes adjust. With great care, he lifts me from my wheelchair and sets me on the bed. My legs spasm slightly. We both giggle a bit while lying on our backs and gazing up at the dark ceiling. Playfully, he asks, "Where are the stars? Oh, it seems like a cloudy night!" I chime in, "Wait, I see Orion!"

I turn my head to get a close-up view of his face. We are both smiling. Our kiss is gentle, instinctive, like animals greeting each other for the first time. The gentle and quiet exploration, a tentative meeting of noses and lips, turns into a slow, lingering dance that forges a powerful connection. It is a reminder of how physical touch transcends language, communicating in ways words never could. Shu and I give each other a world of complete being.

The time feels stretched out. "Would you like me to give you a massage?" he asks gently. I decide to take a chance. The darkness makes me less self-conscious about my imperfect body, even though it is only a matter of time before he will come to understand my atrophies. I roll onto my stomach and close my eyes. He gently undresses me.

As an athlete, he possesses an intimate knowledge of muscles and of the techniques of massage. He starts from my head and works down to my toes, his fingers expertly detecting my stiffness. The touch of his hands is both soothing and intimate and I surrender to the moment. I also notice his unique breathing technique and sense his complete concentration and care. My body is melting, like cooked noodles, all tension draining away.

"Thank you," I say, genuinely grateful. "I know you had a long, busy day and now you're doing this for me. I truly appreciate it."

"It's an honour for me to be able to give you what you need," he replies gently. "Enjoy this moment, and don't let your worries spoil it."

I am fully aware of the preciousness of this experience. How many more massages like this will I be lucky enough to have? At that, I fully embrace it, knowing that I will cherish this beautiful memory forever. I can proudly say, "*Carpe Diem*. Yes, I seized the day."

SLINGSHOTS

"He'll be like a slingshot!" My trusted girlfriend exclaims, her smile filled with assurance. She continues, "I am genuinely excited for you. This is your moment to take control and embrace total freedom in your life. You should express your gratitude to Maya for shielding you, primarily as a mother, up until now. She's created an opportunity for you. Don't view him as your ultimate destiny. Instead, see him as the catalyst for your awakening."

I chuckle at her upbeat and humourous take on the situation. But, at her words, a cloud of guilt and shyness lifts. I picture a slingshot, drawn back and aimed at an apple on a tree. I smile and say, "I hadn't thought about my new life that way. I should thank my daughter who is now carefree!" I really mean it. Even though I am far from the perfect mother, I have raised an amazing daughter.

I contemplate the symbolism of the slingshot and its implications for taking control in this and any future relationships. My girlfriend, a master of communication, put it this way: "You can express it as, 'I would like to have a partner one day and want to find the right person.'" The phrase, whether or not it is entirely true, feels like the ideal way to articulate my unfulfilled desires. Until I met Shu, the idea of a lifelong partner never crossed my mind. Perhaps it may be this new empty-nest status. I had convinced myself that I would be better off being alone, finding companionship in close friendships, and in deepening a connection with my art. But was this the truth? Or was it a carefully constructed defense against my deepest insecurity—the fear of squandering my freedom and potential?

Navigating life while paralyzed from the chest down is a monumental challenge, one that I confront daily. It extends far beyond the complexities of intimate relationships; it encompasses the core of my quality of life. I've had some people interested in me since my divorce (even after I started using a wheelchair), but I often found myself subconsciously building walls, driven in part by a fear of vulnerability and true intimacy. The confines of my chair have fostered a sense of passivity, a feeling that clashes sharply with my true self. Is this some kind of cosmic joke to stop me from being too wild? Or maybe it's supposed to make me realize that looks aren't everything? Before I can reconcile my self-image with the reality of my life, I need to understand my own desires. Why this yearning for a partner? What does it mean to evolve as a single, empty-nester mother? How can I possibly juggle the competing demands of my writing, my community organizing, the need for a life of my own (to truly live!), and the desire to be seen as credible and sincere by others, but more importantly by myself?

In moments of chaos or doubt, I seek solace in the wisdom of my culture. In Japanese tradition, a person of character is often perceived as one who harmonizes opposing forces, much like the interplay of yin and yang. The Japanese proverb "A life is pure and muddy" aptly encapsulates the philosophy and approach embraced by individuals of strong character. I feel deeply connected to this concept and permit myself to apply it to my life after Maya, despite my uncertainty about the practical implications. I realize that I can be both sensual and spiritual, soft-hearted and cautious, serious and playful, loving and cool, emotional and resilient, and, yes, even occasionally mischievous. I can be myself, all of me. I can practice slingshots.

LIFE'S PURSUITS

"I must be brutally honest about what I want," Shu confesses, the subject turning to his risky passion for flying. The morning after another sleepover, we are in my kitchen, coffee in hand, as he talks about small planes, paragliding—the whole thing. He's a competitive flyer, a champion, and he's willing to risk his life for it. Indeed, he reveals now that he has had two near-fatal accidents.

I can't hide my confusion regarding his passion. I respond strongly: "If I had experienced a near-fatal accident, I wouldn't dare return to the skies."

With a grin, Shu counters, "You've got to get back on the horse! Soaring in the skies like a bird is incredible. You don't think about anything when you're up there." He extends his arms and tilts, resembling an eagle in flight, his eyes bright with enthusiasm. I chuckle as I watch his action-packed style of storytelling.

We had cuddled again the previous night—just cuddling, nothing more. However, this night our embrace lingers a bit longer. As I notice the faint scent of his cologne on my skin, I wonder: What trace did I leave on *his* senses? I quickly return to our conversation.

"I wish I had something like that in my life right now... something worth risking my life for," I confess. Another voice within me muses about what might have happened if I hadn't abandoned my research career. And what if I had been more committed to rehabilitation, to trying harder to "reverse" my paralysis? What if my physical well-being had been a greater priority? What if I could somehow have saved my previous marriage?

Then I realize that dwelling on these unproductive questions isn't beneficial, and I redirect my thoughts.

My daughter has been my anchor, my motivation, and my reason for living. Her love and support have sustained me throughout my life with paralysis, just as my love and support have sustained her. This is an undeniable truth. Every decision, from choosing research topics for my community work to organizing intergenerational potlucks, was made with her well-being and future in mind. My life was dedicated to building her brighter tomorrow. My protective instinct, like a cheetah's, always put her first. Just like a mother cheetah instinctively protects her legs by avoiding a fight with other carnivores so she can hunt for her cubs, I've avoided risking my health for Maya.

However, lately, a sense of distance has crept in. I find myself yearning for her company, or even just for a text exchange. Even these have become less frequent. I feel... unneeded. However, I know this is likely a temporary phase in the mother–daughter relationship, much like the phase my mother and I experienced.

After Shu leaves in the morning, I indulge in a long, hot shower to awaken myself. I have slept only four hours instead of my usual six. I stayed awake and, after our cuddling, discreetly moved from the guest-room bed to my own, ensuring I had ample time in case I needed to use the bathroom. It is a topic I haven't discussed with him in depth as I feel embarrassed. The last thing I want is an inadvertent accident. I am like Cinderella at the stroke of midnight and must rush from his embrace.

In the shower, my mind begins to wander. Time is fleeting, and there are so many unexplored paths. I think of my eighty-seven-year-old father back in my hometown in Japan. He has always given me comfort and unwavering support. I am reminded of a poignant conversation we had a year after my mother's passing. "Keiko, what do you think if I were to find a partner, if I could?" he asked over the phone.

Although taken aback, I replied in a warm, gentle tone, "Yes, Dad, if that's what you want. How would you like to find her? Perhaps a cooking class?" I sensed his loneliness, realizing he is, indeed, a man. I couldn't help but wonder how my mother might have reacted in similar circumstances. Now, unexpectedly, I find myself in a somewhat similar position, yearning for a partner. I feel like calling my father and seeking reassurance. But I must first confront my own heart: is a life partner what I truly want?

The steamy bathroom envelopes me like a sauna, making my body feel lighter. In my mind, I compile a list:

1 Spend time with people who make me laugh and feel loved.

2 Continue writing from the heart.

3 Revisit playing the piano and learn to compose music and lyrics.

4 Cultivate a habit of reading books regularly.

5 Do more activities with and for young people.

A harvest moon appears in the night sky. Then, later that day, an unexpected email arrives from Maya's friend Jocelyn. She inquires about my well-being and, to my surprise, suggests we together organize a winter concert, similar to the one I had previously hosted. Jocelyn graciously offers to perform and even suggests other musicians who might join us.

I marvel at the timing. What a delightful coincidence!

OVERTHINKING

As the quiet of the empty nest settles in, I wonder how other single, older women navigate this new chapter, weaving together the threads of solitude, the yearning for romantic connection, and the essential fabric of self-care? The pursuit of love is a fundamental human drive, but it's

FALLING BLOSSOMS
watercolour, 11 × 8

As a Japanese person, I am deeply familiar with the concept of impermanence, and I find its beauty most profound when the petals begin to fall. It reminds me of my grandmother's words: "Even the most beautiful things must eventually fade, but their memory will forever remain."

an especially nuanced and challenging journey for those navigating health concerns. Romance is delicate, fleeting, and can vanish without warning.

I often imagine dancing with Shu, even though my dance movements are limited. Lately, however, I feel lost in the dance, more often following without a clear sense of the next phrase of the music. It's not because I'm unwilling to participate, but rather because I fear going against forces that I may not fully comprehend.

On our next date night, he brings a bag containing ground beef, shrimp, and salmon skewers. While we casually converse, he skillfully prepares two plates of perfectly grilled hamburgers, generously seasoned with Montreal spices and Himalayan salt. "My kids aren't feeling well today, so they're with their mother. That's why I could join you tonight," he says with a warm smile while flipping the sizable hamburgers. "You need to eat more protein, Keiko!"

Shu diligently follows a carnivore diet and has insisted I try his hamburgers. I curiously sample them. It has been years since I ate ground beef, but the beef that evening is delicious, awaking a forgotten hunger within me. Afterward, we watch a documentary on regenerative farming. As the documentary ends, he tenderly places his arm around my shoulder, and I gently settle my right hand on his thigh. Everything up to then has been a novelty, even just cooking together and enjoying a movie. Now we are dancing together. I can feel the rhythm of his breathing. My own breath seems to synchronize with his, deepening our connection. *Is this still dating?* I wonder. I imagine my dopamine and oxytocin levels surging.

By the time bedtime arrives, I know he will be staying. He appeared fatigued during the film and even dozed off at one point.

"I'll meet you upstairs!" I say cheerfully and enter the elevator, my heart racing. As usual, I first go to the washroom. Then, I just want to... not think so much. Imagine just deciding things, no overthinking. What freedom that would be. Without finding an answer, I decide to indulge in the warmth of cuddling. I know that I will have to leave the bed before nature calls.

In the darkness, he tenderly lifts me from the chair and carefully sets me on the bed. I feel strangely weightless in his arms. We exchange a tender goodnight kiss, and my head rests on his muscular arms, my cheek against his scented skin. His left hand supports my side, and he gently lifts my left leg and places it on his. Now I am cradled in the warmth of his skin and the comfort of his presence, held securely in his embrace. The soothing rhythm of his deepening breath soon fills the room. I feel profoundly safe being so close to him.

Sleep eludes me as I luxuriate in my sensations, acutely aware of time. Reluctantly, I turn slowly towards him and plant a gentle kiss on his cheek, whispering, "I'll be back." I don't specify when, but I know I must retreat to my own space for sleep and then return in the early morning to awaken together. He responds with a soft "Okay. Sorry for waking you up" as I hurry to leave. It is 2:00 AM.

I sleep soundly in my own bed. I have a vivid dream in which I visit my childhood house and a heavy, mist-like cloud envelopes me as my home becomes submerged in water. This jolts me awake, leaving me pondering the symbolism of the cloud and the water.

It's 5:00 AM. In the bathroom, I consider my options. Should I go back?

I snuggle back in next to him and sleep until eight in the morning. As the sunrise paints a warm, red circle through my curtains, I turn to look at him, taking in his refined features: his neatly trimmed beard and mustache, the strong lines of his chest, and the scattering of freckles across his tanned shoulders. An impulse seizes me, I softly touch his cheek the way my cat nudges me in the morning. "*Ohayō*!" I whisper. He turns towards me, his eyes half-open, and playfully greets me with, "Good morning! You look like a cat!"

BEGINNING OF THE ENDING

"You are so wonderful," I whisper, cuddling closer.

"You need to be careful," Shu whispers back.

Perplexed and taken by surprise, I ask, "What do you mean, 'I need to be careful'?"

Shu's reply suggests he is only being protective. "Last time you mentioned you were falling for me. Be cautious not to fall hard. I've been trying to shield you from getting hurt. I treat you like a delicate orchid." His words stir a pang in my chest. He is clearly advising me against rushing into deep emotional involvement.

I consider his warning, then respond, "Did I really say that? Well, feelings can change." My words are tinged with both innocence and a touch of defensiveness.

He continues, "We might spend the rest of our lives together, or we might not. I only think of now. Otherwise, we'll miss this precious moment," he says, squeezing my shoulder with his strong hands. His words, focused on the present, clash with my internal turmoil.

Gently, he adds, "I don't know where I'll be in the future. I don't want you to be hurt."

"I know, and I'm glad we talked about it," I say, nestling my head against his arm. My feelings for him are more transparent than I'd thought. I do not know what to do next. While he seems certain about what he wants, I am floundering. I wish I could offer something witty and clever.

Earlier in the day, we enjoyed an art festival, then shared a lovely dinner and a bottle of wine. His broad smile stayed in my memory. Later that evening, we shared stories about past relationships. While he was speaking, my thoughts kept wandering to how dashing he looked at the art show.

The following morning, I prepare my coffee and wait for him to wake up. I am awash with mixed emotions, realizing that this might be the beginning of the ending. I consciously remind myself that I can change, adapt, and embrace.

I'm drawn to his high energy, his ability to communicate so effectively, and the honesty he brings to even the most nuanced discussions. In contrast, I see myself as unsure about what I want, struggling to articulate my thoughts and emotions. His "take it or leave it" approach is not what I have experienced in past relationships. If I accept his terms, how I can protect my emotions? Will my heart and actions be at odds? If his commitment is half-hearted, what choices do I have?

The advice from my girlfriend comes back to me, "You have nothing to lose as a mature, independent woman. Be courageous and voice your desires." Should I accept this level of commitment? Or should I walk away? The sense of an impending deal-breaker weighs on my mind.

TRUSTING

On Sunday, intermittent rain showers grace the day. I comfort myself by immersing once again in the novel *Perfume* by Partick Süskind, and in Maya's notes. The story, while still captivating, holds a darker, more sinister edge than I recall. I miss her terribly, but she is there, alive in the book.

I feel buoyant throughout the day, remembering my conversation with Shu and the fleeting nature of our relationship. I will not let my emotions overpower me. I've accepted things as they are for now. I trust in life and in myself. Reading a book is a way to regain my equilibrium after turbulence, and it is working. As I smile at Maya's brilliant ideas and unfiltered emotions, I am transported into the world of the story.

Occasionally, my thoughts wander toward Shu. Am I falling in love, or out of love? I feel a surprising sense of peace amidst the uncertainty. Why am I this calm? Can I just stay like this? Forever?

That evening, around 8:00 PM, my phone rings. It's Shu. "Hi, I'm on my way back from the airport and just turning onto 33rd Avenue. I'm so close. Would it be possible to come over and see you tonight?" The unexpected call is a delightful surprise, a sudden shift in the evening's peaceful rhythm. "Sure, see you soon!" I say and hang up then hurry upstairs to change out of my T-shirt and make myself more presentable. After ten minutes, he arrives.

He appears in a good mood.

"Why don't we watch a film tonight?" I suggest.

"Yes!" he enthusiastically seconds.

I continue, "Have you seen any work by Hayao Miyazaki, the Japanese director of Studio Ghibli? If you haven't, the films are available on Netflix."

His eyes light up as he responds, "Sure, we can watch Japanese anime! Have you ever heard of Graham Hancock? I've been wanting to watch the series where he visits archaeological sites around the world."

I vaguely remember how passionately he spoke about lost civilizations when we first met. "Sure, that sounds fascinating!" I reply.

He beams and exclaims, "Yes, yes, yes, to the movies, to maybe both films!"

This time, we decide to watch a movie on the laptop while snuggled together in bed—a novel shared experience for both of us. *Ancient Apocalypse* is truly mind-blowing, even if I am not fully convinced. All the information is entirely new to me. I ask him questions throughout the show, and he is genuinely excited to share his insights. It makes the experience even more engaging. "Aren't we like an old couple?" I tease as we sit side by side, completely engrossed in the film. I realize that we have only met about a month ago.

After watching two episodes, we call it a night. We share a tender kiss, turn off the light, and cozy up. His hand finds a comfortable place on my thigh; soon he drifts off to sleep. I close my eyes and catch a little more sleep.

The following morning, as he prepares to leave for the day, we engage in light conversation.

"I often try to discern the underlying meanings behind words," he shares.

"I'm a bit scared, you know," I jokingly reply, "because sometimes it feels like you can see through my emotions with X-ray vision!"

This brings to mind our recent conversation in which he gently cautioned me against falling too deeply too quickly. However, this time, it clicks. Straightforward, rather than cryptic, is the answer. He brings a unique dynamic to our interactions, possessing an aptitude for deciphering my unintentionally cryptic lines.

PRECIOUS THINGS

Bonne nuit and *oyasumi* with kissing emojis are a sweet ritual, but his photos—of flying, food, kids, even selfies—speak thousands of words, offering precious glimpses into his life. I sometimes send photos of Pumpkin and my watercolours.

THE WHISPER OF THE RED CHERRIES
watercolour, 11 × 8

Red cherries appear in my dream, though I can't recall if I tasted them. Some say they symbolize temptation, others say innocence. This ambiguity mirrors the dream itself—a tantalizing glimpse of something both alluring and elusive.

I remark, "You look happy today!"

His response carries a playful tone: "LOL. Try to smile for the picture, you know?!"

His words from earlier—"We might spend the rest of our lives together, or we might part ways"—resonate in my thoughts, particularly the latter part. I'm an empty-nester, enjoying complete freedom and financial security. He, on the other hand, is still deeply involved in raising his two young children, financially supporting his ex and his family. Our lives are so different. This relationship faces challenges. Still, I am intrigued by the possibility of exploring this connection and discovering what new perspectives and experiences it might bring. Daniel, a trusted friend, colleague, and confidant, offered the same wisdom as my girlfriend: be open to the possibilities, and allow yourself to enjoy the journey.

For our seventh date, I send a text to invite him for Sunday dinner. He responds, "Hey, I may be able to come much earlier. The kids are tired and they're going to rest instead. So, I could be free anytime from now."

It's about 1:30 PM. I'm making final adjustments to the menu: beet purée soup, scalloped potatoes, miso-mayo salmon, kale gomae, seven-grain rice, pickled vegetables, and braised beef tenderloin (which he'll grill).

My heart is brimming with anticipation, like a court woman from *The Tale of Genji* awaiting her lover. I'm so pleased he wants to visit so soon, eager for more time together. But above all, I'm excited to finally have the chance to cook for him. Will he relish my cooking? He adheres to a strict carnivore diet, subscribing to the belief that vegetables contain harmful natural toxins. But he can cheat sometimes.

I glance in the mirror and quickly sweep up the sides of my hair, fastening them with a hair clip. My skin has a radiant glow.

He arrives just as I am finishing the cilantro garnish. From his backpack, he pulls out a 2006 dessert wine that his parents gave him, grinning as he says: "It might taste awful by now. But we can try." We toast with a "Santé!"

and begin our early dinner. There's a special kind of joy in creating a meal for those we hold dear.

ENDING THE WORRY

After three days of silence from Shu, I find myself rehearsing a speech to pre-empt the pain. He is, after all, separated but not divorced—a crucial distinction. He must be occupied with his family, I think.

I'm darkly amused to realize I'm following the belief (in some circles) that women self-destruct after three days alone. It's disheartening to see myself so vulnerable. The more I research the complexities of dating a separated man, the more convinced I become that ending things is the right decision. I crave some external validation, a gentle push, even though I already know the answer in my heart.

My diary becomes a repository for my conflicting thoughts: *Eliminate drama. Pursue what you want! The best years of your life.* And, a softer note: *He will always have a special place in my heart.*

Am I making a premature decision? Or a lifesaving one? How should I tell him? In-person feels right, but a heads-up seems considerate. Maybe I should say, "I've given this a lot of thought and wanted to talk to you in person."

My WhatsApp stays silent. No incoming messages. Can I have completely slipped from his thoughts? Is he in a situation where he can't send a message? I send a brief, neutral message: "What have you been up to?"

Shortly afterward, he sends photos from Delta. He was working on his glider. Strangely, I've come to accept his hobby as a priority in his life. This acceptance, I realize, is my way of showing I care. Just then, the phone rings. "Hey, I'm in Delta. My kids are sick, but I got a break from kid duty tonight. What are you doing? Can I come over?" Hearing his real voice after three days of silence is like rain after a drought. But my mind remains guarded. I need real conversation.

I say, "I'm working right now, but I could take a break and see you for a bit, for sure."

"Are you really *working* working? Are you taking a short break and planning to return to work? Or is it a break for the remainder of the day? There's a big difference."

"I suppose I can finish working. I'm a kind of pushover."

"Yeah, I can twist your arm like rubber!" he jokes.

I remind myself that tonight might present a better opportunity for a real conversation.

Half an hour before he arrives, I hurry upstairs to change clothes and polish my appearance. I was at my computer engrossed in work when he called, and I did not expect visitors. My face seems lackluster, particularly around my eyes.

After getting my hair cut earlier that day, I walked through Kerrisdale to a bookstore for a book signing. Waiting at the flashing traffic light was an elderly woman with a walker, her appearance suggesting she'd seen hard times. She called out to me. "You need someone to cross with," she said. "The light's broken, and drivers won't see you in your wheelchair." Touched by her kindness, I crossed with her, the cars stopping to let us pass.

Later, at a Japanese grocery store, I saw her again. She was buying a single rice ball. She mentioned the broken light to the cashier, then turned and smiled. "Oh," she said, "we meet again." I greeted her. My impatience with the long checkout line was momentarily forgotten. Leaving the store, I headed to the bus stop. There she was again! "If something happens twice, it will happen a third time," goes the Japanese saying. I looked at her more closely. Not "strange," just lonely. She immediately began talking about her recent trip to New York, where her two sons live and work. New York! My curiosity was piqued. She had two sons near my age; the elder was a successful film producer. She'd divorced her Harvard-educated husband (who'd treated her poorly) and now lived alone in Vancouver. She was studying science, pursuing a master's in sociology, but had few friends and limited resources. Sharp and articulate, she recalled names and details effortlessly. Despite her intelligence and resilience, her story saddened me. I couldn't imagine being in her shoes at age seventy. We exchanged numbers; she'd call soon.

In the kitchen now, Shu is busy unloading his groceries and preparing to grill his favourite grass-fed beef steaks. "Did you cut your hair? It looks great!" he exclaims, crossing the kitchen in a flash to gently kiss my lips. As a delightful surprise, he has also brought his famous chocolate fondue, declaring, "I will make this again for you!"

While I watch him cooking, I share the events of my day, especially the three times I ran into that lady, and how it made me think about aging and loneliness. I don't expect much from these little moments but sharing them with him opens up a surprising conversation. We talk about aging, about what makes a life meaningful, and about the things that truly matter. It feels like a conversation I could only have had with a close friend or a family member.

Curious and engaged, he continues to cook. He reminds me, "Remember you said last time, 'the next is my turn!' after my massage?"

"Did I say that? Anyway, I would love to give you a massage tonight." We keep talking, listening, and laughing for at least two hours, all while enjoying our dinner.

At around 8:30, we begin preparing for bed. After dimming the light, I ask him to lie on his stomach. The soft glow reveals the contours of our bodies. I pause for a moment, admiring the lines of his back. A quiet sense of intimacy settles between us. "Where do you feel stiff?" I ask softly, gently placing my hand on his smooth skin. I sit beside him, using one arm to support myself while my other arm and fingers probe his back and neck, employing a kind of shiatsu and pressing deeply on specific points. Guided by his responses, I focus on providing extra care around his neck and lower back.

My long, straight hair brushes against his back with rhythmic movements. The world outside feels silent, leaving us enveloped in a cocoon of tranquility. Time seems to linger as we drift into the realm of pillow talk, sharing stories of our youth, travels, his trip to Kyoto, and his brief, youthful romance with a Japanese hostess.

I ask, "Have you ever read *Memoirs of a Geisha*?"

"No, but this, what we're doing now, is a boy's fantasy being served by Geisha Keiko. I shouldn't get used to it. It's too good!" he jokes.

“I bet I could have been a super geisha in a past life.” I say playfully, “Tell me, how can I bring you more pleasure?”

“Let’s try a role play. I’ll be your master, or more like . . . mmm . . . *daimyō*, having my own Geisha Keiko and ruling the country!”

I smile, accepting his playful challenge.

It is already 12:30, time to sleep. In the quiet darkness, his gentle, sweet voice whispers, “You’re beautiful, Keiko.”

MELANCHOLIC BEAUTY

“Japanese anime are always so sad! The characters are always crying!” Shu exclaims. Earlier that day, he’d been such a support, driving me and my van to my second book launch at the Joy Kogawa House and carrying me inside. And now we are at a modest sushi restaurant in my neighbourhood.

“Yes, but the crying is complex,” I say. “It’s about real sadness and the beauty of things ending, like cherry blossoms falling.” I explain. I am referring not just to anime but also to our relationship. I am understanding that I can accept and embrace, albeit with great sadness, the end of our relationship. I smile to myself, knowing he has no idea what I am talking about, all while I gaze at his kind eyes, amused by his recurring gesture, an innocent scratching of his head.

“I bet you never cry, knowing how tough you are!” I joke.

“Actually, today during your book launch speech, I felt myself almost tearing up,” he says.

AUTUMN RAMBLING
watercolour, 11 × 8

The Musqueam Park path, my oasis, is just a step beyond my door. Given my electric chair, I call it rambling rather than walking. I often find myself alone there and able to fully immerse myself in the natural surroundings and simply "be."

My eyes widen in surprise. "Really!? Which part?"

"Well, some lines after you mentioned your New York friends who read your book with tears... but I forgot the exact lines."

"I see..." I wonder what triggered such emotions in him. Was it something I'd said before? Shu always encodes information somewhere in his brain, and the process of decoding his thoughts is often unexpectedly enlightening. "I would love to see you crying one day!" I tease.

After the two-hour dinner, which ends up being twice as long as originally planned, we drive to my home and decide to watch a Netflix movie. He is in the mood for a rom-com. We settle on *Love Hard,* a Christmas-themed romantic comedy.

During climactic and endearing moments, Shu, scratching his forearm as if he has goosebumps, exclaims and laughs, "Ahhh, I cannot watch it. So stressful and awkward!" He clearly identifies with the main character. I always appreciate his uninhibited emotional responses, a trait born, I suspect, from his low tolerance for suspense, particularly during thrilling and unpredictable scenes.

Enjoying the movie and his reactions, I take his hand. He squeezes gently. I never thought of holding hands as a primary expression of affection, but with Shu, it's different. He always offers his hands, both literally and figuratively. Even when he seems asleep, his hand finds mine, holding me close. I find it romantic, the feeling of shared energy or, as he calls it, microbiome. Germs or not, I feel his love. But the intimacy sparks a familiar sadness. I think of cherry blossoms falling, snowflakes melting—fleeting beauty. This feeling, this connection, I say to myself, is just as fragile.

PILLOW TALK

"Oh, no!" he exclaims, leaping out of bed at 5:00 AM, after my cat wakes him up. He is supposed to leave my place at 4:45 to take his son to a hockey game. Unfortunately, his alarm failed to ring, and his ex is yelling at him over the phone. Without the usual meticulous bed-making or goodbye kisses, he rushes off.

This reignites my doubts. Am I just a distraction? The next few days pass with our usual sporadic texts. I do my best to mask the unease in my heart. Then he texts to inquire about my availability that day. Instead of my usual positive and delighted response, I write, "What's on your mind?" And I vow to indulge him less. Later, we speak over the phone, humorously acknowledging our low energy levels that night and concluding on a tender note.

The next evening, I send a text saying, "How is your day? I missed you a little bit." I don't usually confess I miss him.

He replies, "Woaaa! Not sure if we'll be able to see each other soon, though? Sunday evening may be possible, TBC. *Bonne nuit*, cutie-cat! Xoxo."

His "Woaaa!" is so adorable.

A few days later, we have our usual dinner at my place. We talk and laugh like good friends. Later in bed, he starts singing a song softly. Our pillow talk has become my favourite part of our connection. Shu tenderly asks why I missed him that day, recognizing that such an expression is not my usual. I am intrigued by his keen observation. Nothing escapes his notice. I think he observes the subtle change in my tone and expression.

"Umm, I am holding back, you know, because of our situation," I confess, surprised by my admission of something unpleasant.

"Oh, no. It's not good if you feel burdened," he replies in a kindly but distressed tone. He adds, "If you are looking for something deeper, I may not be able to offer it to you."

That last line of his stings my heart.

"Remember when you said, 'Don't fall from too high or too hard,'" I whisper, nestling my head further onto his shoulder.

He assures me, "I will catch you if you fall."

I am utterly lost for words.

Finally, to redirect the conversation, I exclaim: "I love hearing about your passion for flying. It must be such an exhilarating experience."

He nods. "Flying, to me, feels like a marvel of modern invention, seamlessly blending science and art. The sensation of becoming one with the wind is truly remarkable." Then, he adds, "If I obtain permission from the club, I'd like to take you up in a passenger seat next summer."

"I might need a will!" I joke. Then, more sincerely, I say: "Regardless, I'd love to cheer you on during your flights." I picture us flying together—a dream within a dream.

LUNAR ECLIPSE

Nearly four months have passed since I first met Shu. Our future remains uncertain. Our meet-ups go from a few times a week to once every few weeks. One day, I text him and try for lighthearted tone: "It feels like we are drifting apart. Hope we can have a conversation when you have time. No worries, I totally respect your feelings and circumstances. I like you a lot but just wanted to know if I need to let go."

His response is immediate and lengthy: "Hi, Keiko-kat! You are right. I apologize for being absent lately. I've been using my time off to train on a soaring simulator for an upcoming competition this summer. I'd like to do okay and not embarrass myself but, most importantly, fly safely. This has taken a lot of my brain power and attention, leaving little time for us. Tuesday, Thursday, and Sunday evenings, as well as Saturdays, are when we usually saw each other before... I'm sorry this has left you hanging dry... I don't have much time today. Maybe tomorrow during lunch or sometimes in the evening?"

He also shares details about the online courses he has signed up for and his schedule for online competitions. I wish he had told me earlier about his plans and the reasons why he couldn't see me, but I appreciate his honesty. Something shifts within me. I genuinely hope he will achieve his dreams, even if it means not seeing him anymore.

The following day our video call lasts an hour. He enthusiastically shares his VR gear, describing how it allows him to fly virtually anywhere on earth with incredible realism. The line between real and virtual flying has blurred. The future has arrived. Humans can now experience flight without ever leaving their rooms. I ponder what implications this might hold for human connections and relationships. The thought of Shu donning his VR headset and sitting alone in his dimly lit bachelor suite is unappealing and somewhat troubling.

In the weeks that follow, I find myself enjoying a newfound inner stillness. I am deeply engrossed in my work and in community commitments, and I also am busy reading Murakami's new novel, *The City and Its Uncertain Walls.* Its dreamlike narrative blurs the boundaries between reality and imagination and offers a comforting refuge, a space for contemplation amidst the lingering questions of self, loss, and the elusive nature of existence. Night after night, I return to the pages of the book.

Looking back over the past four months, I realize the extent of my personal growth. Thoughts of him are rare, and the desire to seek out another relationship hardly crosses my mind. It feels like I am emerging from a storm. I wonder what has prompted this shift. Perhaps the physical distance from Shu played a part. Or maybe it's a kind of awakening? Whatever the reason, I feel a profound sense of equilibrium. I find myself chuckling quietly, recalling the Japanese proverb "A woman's heart is like the autumn sky." I'm no exception, it seems, my emotions shifting easily, unpredictably, like the ever-changing clouds of an autumn sky. I picture the harvest moon, its enchanting glow waxing and waning through its phases. I see the waning moon casting its shadow.

I silently and wholeheartedly thank Shu for our brief but meaningful encounters, a bright spot during this difficult time of empty nesting.

All this brings to mind a remarkable documentary I'd recently seen about a rogue lioness in Kenya. Rejected by her pride and grieving the loss of her cubs, she'd defied all instincts and attempted to adopt a baby oryx. It was an unheard-of act, a predator embracing a prey animal in a maternal bond. The scientists believed loneliness had fueled this unusual love. The baby oryx, overcoming its initial fear, had instinctively tried to nurse, though the lioness's milk never came. Eventually, the baby oryx rejoined her real mother, leaving the lioness to search, it seemed, forever.

The lioness's story felt strangely familiar. Was I that lioness, driven by the same powerful mix of motherhood and the unsettling emptiness of the nest? Was I also seeking connection, a new form of belonging? Had I acted out of character? Was it worth the gamble, even with an uncertain outcome? My unexpected connection with Shu felt like a gift, a mystery bestowed by fate.

As we pass through life, shedding the labels of youth—desirable woman, partner, mother—our roles must transform if we are to embrace what's next. The shadow-self whispers: Who do I want to be now? Is the pull of motherhood too deeply ingrained to transcend? What lessons can I learn from the lone lioness's story, from nature's mysteries? How can I evolve while staying true to myself? I turn to the moon's phases, a timeless compass for women, a luminous symbol of perpetual change, cyclical rebirth, and the ever-shifting tides of life.

I may encounter him again, or I may not. There may be periods when I find myself alone. I may date someone else. I am a sky full of moons, a constellation of dreams, and I choose which ones to let shine—each a chapter waiting to be written.

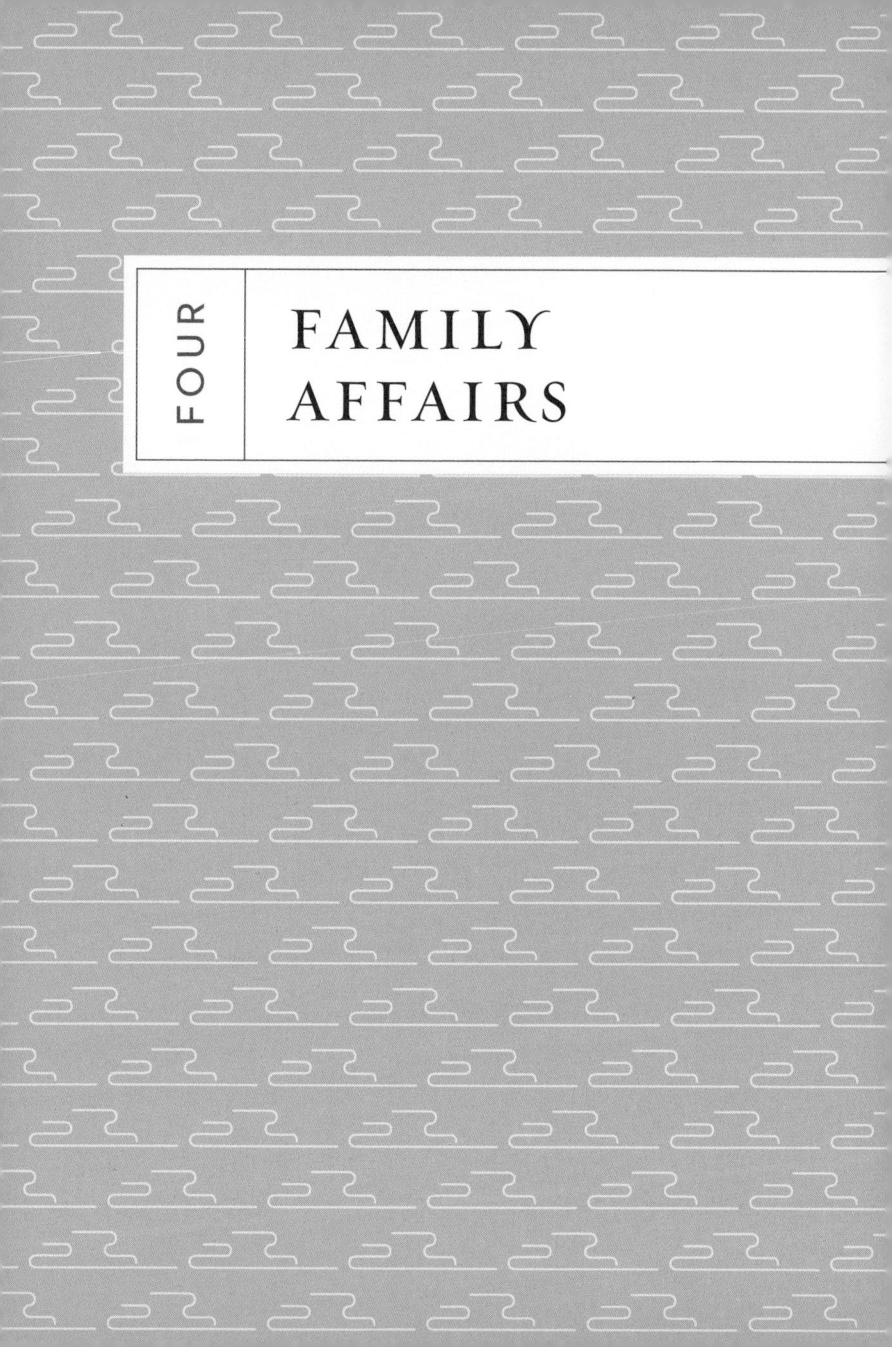

FOUR

FAMILY AFFAIRS

MY BELOVED FATHER'S WISH
watercolour, 9 × 12

For his eighty-seventh birthday, I painted a portrait of my beloved father, Goro Honda. I strove to capture his essence, his meticulousness, his unwavering patience, and his wonderful sense of humour. I mailed the original to Japan, where it now hangs proudly on my mother's altar. He adored it, saying it truly resembled him. He often expressed his desire to live a long and fulfilling life, to support his two daughters, three grandchildren, and one great-grandchild. He believed this would bring immense joy to my mother in heaven. I am incredibly fortunate to have had such a remarkable father.

家、家にあらず。継ぐをもて家とす。

A family does not endure
unless the art of
performance is passed down.

ZEAMI MOTOKIYO

ACCORDING TO ZEAMI, the renowned Noh theorist, a family line endures not only through biology but also through the faithful transmission of artistic mastery. I wonder if this is truly the case in my family, or if there are some other forms of artistry that define our legacy. Stars are thought to be the souls of ancestors in Japanese belief. If they are, what stories would they have to tell? And if they are trying to tell me something, how should I listen?

The world of Noh is a world of masks, each one unique and expressive. Noh performers believe these masks possess a power that transcends their physical form, imbuing them with a spiritual significance. While often described as having neutral expressions, they are, in fact, meticulously crafted to convey a range of emotions. I had the privilege of wearing a Noh mask carved by Yayoi Hirano, a celebrated Japanese artist and Noh mask carver residing in Vancouver.

The experience followed an interview I conducted with her for *Kerrisdale Playbook*, the community e-zine I created for the Kerrisdale Community Centre Society. She brought a diverse collection, showcasing masks of young men, old men, women, and even demonic figures. Yayoi-san kindly let me try one on, and I selected a laughing old man mask with bears at the sides. The excitement and almost reverent feeling of that novel experience remains vivid in my memory. I felt the weight of history. Did it change me, even in some small way? Maybe yes. I wonder if that experience planted the seed of my fascination with Zeami's concept of the hidden flower.

MY MOTHER'S URN

My father's voice comes softly through the phone, "I will bring your mother's ashes when I come to Vancouver next month, so please arrange with your sister to select an urn for the ashes."

I purchased business class plane tickets for my father to attend Maya's graduation in June. He has been here before, but this time he will make the journey alone, without the company of my mother. At eighty-seven years old, my father travelling alone from overseas causes anxiety for both of us. It has been five years since we last saw each other in person. My excitement is hard to contain. I also wish to get a portion of my mother's ashes from him to create my unique urn (骨壷, *kotsu-tsubo*) and Buddhist altar (仏壇, *butsudan*) in my Vancouver home.

My sister sends me a link to a business site that sells portable-sized urns. I take a quick look, but I find the designs grotesque; some look like a fortune teller's crystal ball. Others exude a religious aura. I am also disheartened by the extravagant prices. Most urns are priced over 10,000 yen, roughly 100 dollars. "Can I research a bit more and choose one?" We converse on LINE, the family messaging app.

I choose an elegant tea canister. It is decorated with exquisite purple washi paper that is accented with shimmering silver flecks.

Beyond its aesthetic appeal, it boasts impeccable craftsmanship, featuring a secure seal, all at a reasonable cost of 1,000 yen (10 dollars). It is also unbreakable, adding to its allure. I pat myself on the back for the brilliant choice. The choice of purple is special and significant, being my mother's favourite colour. I purchase it through Amazon Japan, and have it sent directly to my father. I also send the picture of it to my uncle, Tetsurō. He replies in brief, "Nice choice!"

I inform my father and sister of my selection and alert them about the impending Amazon delivery, but I receive no response from either of them for some time. Uh-oh! Something seems amiss. Puzzled, I tap the reply button on LINE to gently remind them about my decision.

My sister's response takes me by surprise: "Please reconsider your choice. It's shocking that you're even contemplating using a tea canister for Mom's ashes." She adds, "Our father is very disappointed with you."

I fire back, "What's wrong? What's wrong with me choosing my own altar at which I will be the sole worshipper? Do we need to pick one that is *commercially* labeled as an urn?"

She calmly replies, "Please consider our father's feelings."

I am perplexed by what she means, as I have no idea yet what he is thinking. Feeling anxious, I call him, inadvertently escalating the situation.

"It is utterly disrespectful," he declares. "And you cannot put ashes in a steel or plastic container. It must be porcelain." It seems he has made up his mind even before hearing my perspective.

I counter, "When I was researching, I found many commercially labeled urns made of steel and plastic. What about those?"

"If you're not listening, then I won't bring your mother's ashes to you." With that, we hang up.

Feeling upset and frustrated, I turn to my confidant, my uncle Tetsurō, to vent about the situation and present all my reasons and carefully researched choices via our video chat.

"You seem to be very upset, which is unnecessary," Uncle Tetsurō says. "Just listen to your dad. Keiko, you are so passionate. This is one of your most attractive traits, but it also reminds me of your mother. Seriously!" he laughs, referring to her stubbornness. He concludes with a smile. After our brief conversation, he sends me a link, saying, "Just check it out!" The link leads to the website of a company that offers more refined and stylish urns, including a lovely, unadorned one of Japanese cypress wood.

Talking to Tetsurō helps me regain composure and allows me to see things from my father's and sister's perspectives, prompting a reflection on my cultural evolution. I have been living outside of Japan for so long, and sometimes I find the Japanese concept of *kūki wo yomu* (reading the air) a bit convoluted. I now seem disconnected from my father and sister. Am I being insensitive to their cultural norms and traditions? It could be they dislike how my individualistic approach to ancestor worship deviates from the traditional Japanese ways, or perhaps they disagree with my preference for practicality over symbolic value. Or, more likely, it is my admittedly biased perspective on the Japanese cultural imperative of saving face, *mentsu wo tamotsu,* that grates against their sensibilities?

In any case, I decide to bridge the gap by seeking my father's opinion on the plain cypress wood urn option.

"Oh, this looks really nice," he responds, surprisingly, as if the argument had never occurred. He even adds, as if he has read my mind: "You can personalize it as you wish." My sister is very happy to hear that we have reached an agreement that has surpassed both her suggestion and my original selection. I reflect that it has been a distressing but ultimately worthwhile process to find the perfect urn for my mother.

PASSING A TORCH

"Good morning, Dad!" I eagerly wait to hear his voice on the LINE app, having just sent him the newest space heater for his eighty-seventh birthday. It is already 8:00 AM in Japan. He picks up the phone by his bed, "Oh, how are you?" His face appears upside down again.

I laugh. "Dad, I only see the top of your shiny head that is upside down!" He still has not figured out how to fix his smartphone setting. "Did you open the present? Did you start using it?" I ask.

"Thanks, Keiko. I opened it, but it says 1,500 watts, and this house doesn't have the capacity for it unless I upgrade the entire electrical wiring. Can return it? Also, it says 27,000 yen, so it's quite expensive and would be wasteful if I don't use it." He pauses, then says, "Could you please let me know before you send something like this?" Unlike the last time, when he expressed frustration and sharp disapproval over a similar situation, he is carefully choosing his words and his tones. My father is becoming a wise old man, I think.

"Hmm, well, I knew you would say that. That's why I did not want to give you a heads-up beforehand. But I think it's totally worthwhile trying to use it, as this type has four different levels of electric power adjustment. Read the manual, so you know what I am talking about!" I suggest brightly.

He agrees, his response surprisingly receptive and considerate. I always aim to catch him in the morning while he is half awake and still in bed. He continues, "You are like me, always saving and not spending your money for yourself. But, Keiko, please spend more on yourself, but leave just enough for your final years of life."

"I know, Dad, and thank you. I'll try to change and explore new parts of the world in the coming months and years." I reply, the words flow smoothly, yet I know my risk-averse nature makes such a change unlikely.

"Keiko, travel to Europe, or South America, or wherever you feel like going. You can spend a lot of money on hiring people and flying business class, and you can still feel secure about your finances. So, no worries, please. While you can still move and feel energetic, this is the time to do it. Don't wait until your last remaining days," he continues. His voice is passionate and convincing.

He adds, "I really respect your capability, Keiko. You are always surrounded by people who care about you and come all the way to your house to visit you all the time. Who else would have such fortune? You look exceptionally young because of your indomitable spirit and your enduring effort, I know. So, I have full confidence that you can expand yourself more and I strongly encourage you to travel more."

After absorbing his passionate words, my heart brims with hope, love, possibilities, and excitement—emotions I liken to the Japanese expression *waku waku*, which evokes the thrill of falling in love or diving into a cherished new book. Strikingly, my late uncle, Tetsurō, when in his early seventies, used the very term *waku waku* when reigniting his passion for playing his guitar. How blessed I am to have a father who not only intimately understands my nature but also motivates me with his unwavering support and love. I am flooded with profound happiness. Won over by his smiling face and his tender voice on my iPhone, I reflect on his humble nature. I think of the stories he often shares about his childhood during the war.

My father, born in Tokyo in 1936, was one of the hundreds of thousands of children evacuated to the countryside during the Second World War. At the age of seven, he and his mother were separated from his father, who worked at the Yasuda Bank in Tokyo, and were sent to live with distant relatives in Kumamoto City, my hometown.

He once told me that when he was eight years old, he and his classmates were instructed by their teacher to build a giant aircraft using bamboo and paper. This was displayed on the school grounds to deceive American pilots into believing that Japan still had the capacity to fight. As a child, he found the idea absurd and useless, but he had to follow orders.

Growing up in the city, he was unfamiliar with the natural world and struggled to adapt to the climate of Kumamoto. His delicate skin was constantly bitten by insects, and he often missed the conveniences of city life. What struck me most about his poignant story was the profound loneliness he experienced and his sense of not belonging. He often spent his days playing alone in the fields, being miserable and feeling like a burden to his host family. His mother also faced challenges adjusting to rural life. They both persevered.

Even today, my father has a fondness for bananas, a luxury back then. His resilience and gratitude are a testament to the challenges he faced. Every time I visualize the young boy he once was, I feel a deep sense of respect and compassion.

My father's frugal nature, evident in his reluctance to upgrade his space heater, is a reminder of the tough times he went through as a child.

After we hang up, I write down my goals, envisioning where I want to be in five years and reverse-engineering the steps I need to take in the next six months. I scour the world map, seeking independent bookstores that are selling my freshly published debut memoir. My focus shifts to bookstores in New York City, Toronto, Portland, Phoenix,

Long Beach, Seattle, and Bern in Switzerland. Connecting with a future audience through my art and embracing new ideas will be my source of excitement, my *waku waku.* I will need to draw on my inner strength to confront the looming logistical challenges of travelling with a wheelchair and needing a travel companion.

The remembrance of my father's encouragement along with a mix of nervousness and excitement, carries me through the late night. I am standing on my parents' shoulders, carrying their torch.

MY UNCLE'S FINAL TEACUP: *KONKONCHIKI*

My dear uncle Tetsurō, with whom I grew up and whom I considered my closest friend, passed away just a few days before his seventy-fifth birthday, right before Maya and Micah were set to leave for Japan. He was a self-taught artist and was proficient in oils, acrylics, and watercolours, just like his father had been. He was also an amateur guitarist, often performing his original compositions. On October 2, 2022, a little over a year before his passing, my close friend, Armenian-born pianist and composer Gerard Satamian, performed my uncle's original song, *A Song of Memories,* at The Opera Zone, a music performance series I co-founded with Gerard in 2016. As chair of the Community Engagement Committee of the Kerrisdale Community Centre (KCC) board, I'd started The

THE ARTIST
watercolour, 9 × 12

"I never imagined experiencing such excitement again after turning seventy," my beloved uncle Tetsurō confessed, "until I picked up a guitar again." He was my hero and closest confidant, cultivating his inner world and expressing it through his art. I miss him dearly.

Opera Zone with him and other collaborating musicians after a casual conversation about his passion for opera and the desire for a free community space for both artists and community members. It's a cherished monthly program that's still going strong. When Tetsurō initially shared his guitar composition and song lyrics with me, I immediately asked Gerard to arrange it for piano, hoping to play and sing along myself. The song was a beautiful tribute to his parents, my beloved grandparents, who also hold a special place in my heart. Gerard's arrangement was exquisite. I recorded his piano performance at the community centre and shared it with Tetsurō and the rest of my family. I still vividly remember Tetsurō's surprised and happy face. What a precious memory!

Tetsurō also immersed himself in the art of fly fishing, meticulously tying feathered flies, and pursued numerous other hobbies throughout his life. During his university days, he joined the student movement against war and other injustices. He had a principled spirit much like his father, Konosuke, my maternal grandfather.

About a week before his passing, even as he faced the final stages of cancer, Tetsurō decided to create an original ceramic cup to bequeath to all his family members as his final legacy. Using hiragana script, he inscribed the unfamiliar Japanese word こんこんちき (*konkonchiki*) in his own handwriting on the plain, white mug, accompanied by a child-like drawing of man's legs in bright blue with four grey dots placed before the word.

I hold my cup and grin. "He did it again!" I exclaim, captivated by the cryptic letters and drawings. He imparted philosophical lessons throughout my life. I had never heard of the word *konkonchiki* before, and I wonder what it means. It strikes me as very cool for him to leave something so mysterious for us to decipher. Is there a hidden message or a challenge for me to unravel? His kind voice echoes in my mind, saying, "Keiko, see what you can come up with!"

I respond aloud, "Yes, I accept your challenge." But I am feeling puzzled.

Naturally, I google the word. I am amazed by its complexity. In the Edo dialect, *konkonchiki* originally referred to a fox. The reason for this remains unclear, but the word's sound might have played a significant role. Used at the end of a sentence, *konkonchiki* inflects the preceding word, much like the phrase "of course!" in English. When directed at a person, it can either be playfully teasing or insulting, depending on the context, making it versatile. I wonder if my uncle was poking fun at himself. The many connotations of the word *konkonchiki* leave me intrigued and perplexed. I wish I could have discussed it with him; but then I realize that he had intentionally left me with a puzzle to solve.

I question why I feel compelled to take on these challenges. The answer remains elusive. Nevertheless, he holds a significant place in my life, and I long to grasp the essence of his being. Perhaps it is about glimpsing the vast potential of humanity.

In July 2022, exactly a year before he died, Tetsurō underwent stomach cancer surgery, resulting in the removal of two-thirds of his stomach. When he was discharged, he sent me a voice message. His voice was faint, unlike anything I'd heard before. He said, "*Kyō*... *taiin*... *shimashita,*" meaning, "I am discharged today." I listened to his message multiple times to truly appreciate his effort and determination, and this only brought my heart closer to him.

After reading a research article published by a group of Japanese scientists that emphasized the potent inhibitory effects of petasin—found in butterbur sprouts—on cancer proliferation and metastasis, I began sending Tetsurō butterbur sprouts to include in his post-surgery diet. I was not certain about their efficacy, but I clung to hope. Following his surgery, he texted me, saying, "I drink the power of butterbur sprouts every day. Thank you. I'm truly grateful for your support." Our regular video calls and text exchanges continued as usual, at least once every other week.

One day, Tetsurō mentioned, "I've decided to keep a two-year journal instead of three-year one." I shared a memory of my mother buying a three-year diary, to which he responded, "Three years sounds like a lot, but two years feels manageable. I'm only jotting down a few sentences. That's it!"

"I see!" I replied. "That doesn't sound overwhelming. Please keep writing, so one day I'll get to read it. It will be our family treasure!"

During our conversation, I sensed a dark undercurrent, almost like a chill running down my spine. As we discussed the two-year diary, I wondered about his thoughts and physical condition. Subsequently, he shared with me the news of the cancer's metastasis. I was utterly shocked, recalling the moment I received similar news about my mother's cancer. My mindset swiftly shifted to valuing every precious minute and second spent with him, and to recognizing the need to prepare for the coming separation.

Sadly, my uncle Tetsurō passed away on July 7, 2023. He never held my debut memoir, *Accidental Blooms*, in his hands nor saw the book cover he had praised. He was a significant figure in my life—my hero, best friend, and co-conspirator. He ignited my love for pattern recognition and making sense of things.

Early in my epidemiology career, I often found myself confined to conventional thinking, sometimes missing the deeper truths hidden in the outliers. But then, after I began using a wheelchair, I became an outlier myself. And I found myself drawing on the creative thinking skills he had nurtured in me since childhood. Would he ever receive the credit he deserved?

Tetsurō included his poem titled「コンコンチキ」("*Kon-konchiki*") in his two-year diary. After his death, his widow, Minako, kindly shared a few pages from his diary and gave me permission to include it in my future book. I was aware that Tetsurō wrote poems not just for himself but also his family, much like my grandfather, whose poetry is cherished and lovingly preserved as a source of heartfelt connection within our family.

コンコンチキ
Konkonchiki

by Tetsurō Masuda

病み上がりで痩せ細り　こんな僕でもコーヒーは
豆から引いてくつろいで　想いにふけるひと時よ
甘い思いにギーターを手に　昔懐かし弾き語り
指は動かず手は痛く　哀れなるかコンコンチキ

歩くと傾きふらふらで　ゴアのパーカースニーカー
気取ってみても所詮は はげた頭の御老人
思い直してハットを被り　昔懐かし町家の通り
ショーウインドウのガラスには　哀れなるかなコンコンチキ

Ill and thin from recovery,
Even in this state, coffee brewed from beans
Brings comfort and contemplation,
A sweet reverie, with a guitar in hand,
Nostalgically strumming and singing.
Fingers still, hands in pain,
A pitiful *Konkonchiki*.

Walking with a wobbly gait,
Wearing Gore's Parker sneakers,
Even if I try to look cool,
I'm just an old man with a bald head.
I reconsider and put on my hat,
Strolling through the nostalgic old town street,
In the shop window's glass, I wonder,
Oh, the pitiful sound of *Konkonchiki*.

On the same page, there is also a statement that truly captivates me: 自分に真面目なコンコンチキでありたい。ん、どう言うこと？今の自分の正直なところがよくわからない。(I want to be an honest *Konkonchiki* to myself. Hmm, what does that mean? I'm not sure about the true nature of myself right now.) *Konkonchiki* remained a mystery to me, continually sparking my curiosity about how to uncover our true selves. One day, after sharing the story of my uncle's final cup with my artist friend, Jamie, he looked at the cup and said, "Isn't that the symbol in Japanese characters meaning, a human being,?" He pointed to the blue drawing on the cup: 人.

"Oh, my god! I hadn't recognized it! Indeed, it's like the symbol for a human being!!" I exclaimed. Was this by coincidence? Tetsurō proved again that he was a humanist who kept pondering the question of who he was.

His last words to me, during our final video chat a week before he died, perfectly captured who he was. Even as he struggled to breathe, he mustered all his strength to say, "Keiko-chan, nothing to feel sad about. This is a very natural thing."

BENEATH THE WATCHFUL EYES OF A MAN

I distinctly recall one of my phone conversations with Tetsurō during the Covid pandemic. He drew my attention to a specific *tanka* from the poetry collection of my deceased grandfather, Konosuke. *Tanka* is a traditional form of Japanese poetry with a thousand-year-old history.

These poems comprise a five-line structure with a specific syllable pattern: 5-7-5-7-7.

On March 29, 1995, at the age of eighty, my beloved grandmother, Tamiko, was admitted to the hospital for kidney failure in anticipation of dialysis, despite her initial resistance. On April 8, she received a temporary discharge permission for one day to participate in the civic election. My grandfather wrote these two similar soulful and sensual poems on that day when his wife came home from hospital.

相抱く　病の妻は　涙ぐむ
傘寿を迎え 愛を知るわれ

Holding my wife (in bed),
My ailing wife sheds tears.
Welcoming my eightieth birthday,
I come to know love.

相抱く　病の妻は　顔をおい
恥じらいの目は　若き日のまま

Holding my wife (in bed),
My ailing wife covers her face.
Her shy eyes remain,
as they are in her youth.

平成7年4月８日　(April 8, 1995)

"Can you imagine that scene?" Tetsurō said. "I'm fascinated to discover these moments, and I am surprised by the depth of my father's feelings for my mother."

"Indeed," I remarked. "We had never witnessed him embrace her or verbally express love in our presence." I recalled my childhood and sleeping between my grandparents in their futon; they never even held hands. Such open displays of affection were uncommon for a traditional Japanese couple from the Taishō era (1912–1926). Public affection, at home or elsewhere, was considered unsophisticated, undignified, and dishonourable—a breach of their generation's norms.

Tetsurō continued, "I particularly appreciate the phrase 'Her shy eyes remain, as they are in her youth' as it truly captures Tamiko's essence and Konosuke's keen observation."

As I envision my grandfather's state of mind on that day, I feel a warmth within. He saw my grandmother as beautiful and pure as she was in her youth, and he felt as passionate as he did in his younger days. Did they kiss? Did they exchange any words? Did they engage in intimacy? Did their eyes meet? What is it like to embody the sentiment "I come to know love" at the age of eighty? I read that and I get goosebumps.

Loving a partner for a lifetime and embracing the frailty of aging bodies lies beyond my lived experience and imagination. Yet, however elusive it might be to a middle-aged divorcee such as myself, it remains at the centre of my yearning. I ponder whether I will ever find a man who will love me in my very old age the way Konosuke loved his wife. If so, it would be the ultimate fulfillment; if not, my life will still be sweet and wonderful. I try not to worry.

Yet, I can't shake off his words, "I come to know love." How powerful this line is! What he meant is the passionate love between a man and a woman. Or did he mean something else, like an eternal connection? I am not sure; all I can do is try to read between the lines. I sense a significant limitation in the English language to convey the depth of the love my grandfather expressed in his poetry, a feeling we must interpret for ourselves. The term "passionate love" feels insufficient. I wish my uncle was still alive to continue conversing on this topic with me.

The last time I saw my uncle in person was when he and his wife visited me in Vancouver in the fall of 2019, right before the Covid pandemic. On the last day of their stay, my uncle told me, "Keiko, you are still beautiful and able to find a partner again, and you need to take good care of your appearance. So, I will leave my nose-hair trimmer for you to use."

"What?! What do you mean? Do I look so ungroomed?" I burst into laughter. No one, not my ex-husband nor ex-boyfriends, had ever made such a remark. A nose-hair trimmer!

"Just use it!" He tenderly smiled, as usual. I took it as brotherly, unconditional love from a male perspective.

After that, I started paying attention to my nose hairs for the first time in my life! The trimmer brings back that humourous, heartwarming memory every time I use it, but I can't say it changes my appearance. I think that Tetsurō wanted to show his care and insight through actions, not just words, when we said goodbye. That nose-hair trimmer is the only keepsake I received from him and serves as a humourous symbol of our closeness as well as a gentle encouragement to find love, whatever it means.

Tetsurō's nose-hair trimmer, along with my grandfather's poem, are both endorsements of true love, sources of hope—a small but persistent hope.

SPRING WARMTH

There's nothing quite like a morning after the rain when the sun bursts through and the garden plants are adorned with sparkling dewdrops. This scene always stirs an unforgettable memory within me, one from about five years ago.

On a clear spring morning, the large stone in my small Japanese courtyard garden presented a remarkable sight. The morning sun, striking its surface, made it appear as if it were emitting a thin, white, smoke-like vapor, reminiscent of steam rising from a boiling kettle. This stark contrast against the glistening, dew-covered moss surrounding the stone conjured an otherworldly beauty, a small pocket of magic within my own garden.

I opened the window, drawing in a lungful of spring air through the screen. My cat, Pumpkin, joined me, her gaze fixed on the world beyond the mesh. She is my sole companion here. "Such a lovely day," I whispered to her, "but I'm so sorry, you can't go out." In that moment, I saw our shared fate. Like me, she is confined, a bird in a cage. Seemingly free-spirited, yet bound by invisible threads, we live each day with a quiet acceptance. Profound

SPRING ADVENTURE
watercolour, 9 × 12

My cat, Pumpkin, is my teacher and entertainer, capable of portraying a variety of roles, from wise elder to youthful beauty.

affection washed over me. "You must yearn for adventure out there," I said.

Yes, perhaps just a fleeting moment of freedom wouldn't hurt. Prompted by the allure of spring, my hand reached for the screen. And in an instant, Pumpkin was outside.

She moved slowly, close to the ground, cautiously looking around before halting on the moss that was now a shimmering expanse, like a carpet of jewels. With a tender gesture, she brought her face close to the shepherd's purse, a flowering common weed, that grew at the base of the large stone. What secret was she sharing with it? The rising sun, illuminating her from behind, mingled with her soft fur, giving her a radiant glow. A sweet, almost magical stillness surrounded her, and I was spellbound by the extraordinary sight. It seemed to exist outside of reality yet held the essence of nature's truth—a vision of happiness made real, like a painting come to life.

Tears welled up in my eyes. Even if she didn't come back, I decided I wouldn't regret giving her this moment of happiness. "Pumpkin, enjoy yourself," I whispered. "Play with nature, play with your friends." And with that, she disappeared into the depths of the garden.

In that instant, it was if I'd been jolted awake from a dream. My whole body tensed. I felt my heart pounding. My mind went blank. An uncertain future stretched before me. I thought: *What if she doesn't come back? What if she gets hit by a car or is injured somewhere and can't find her way home?* Intense anxiety and regret rushed through me.

Twenty minutes passed like an eternity. I could only stare out at the world, waiting with growing unease. In stark contrast to the beautiful scene I'd witnessed moments before, my mind was now filled with worst-case scenarios. *Where is Pumpkin now?* I wondered. *Is she fearfully crossing the rough asphalt, dodging the passing cars? Has she been startled by the neighbour's big dog? When would she come back? And which window would she use to return?* Including the front door, there were five possible entry points. Though it was spring, I couldn't leave them all open. I could only roam restlessly around the window she'd escaped through.

On impulse, I decided to check the other kitchen window. I opened it and peered out through the screen. In that instant, I heard something rustling beneath the deck. Then, a low, guttural growl, followed by a piercing shriek unlike anything I'd ever heard. The sheer agony of the sound sent a chill through me, as if my blood had turned to ice. A vision seared into my mind: Pumpkin, locked in a desperate struggle with a raccoon under the dark deck, being grievously wounded. The image gripped my heart mercilessly. "Pumpkin! Pumpkin!" I screamed repeatedly out of pure desperation. I could only imagine the alarm my frantic cries caused the neighbours. A terrifying silence rose from beneath the deck.

I clung to desperate but hopeful thoughts: *Pumpkin is alive, she can hear me. But what if she is severely injured, unable to move? What if she is barely breathing, crying for help?*

Oh, I felt so helpless. The guilt of allowing my precious cat to suffer such a fate, combined with the crushing grief of potentially losing her, unleashed a torrent of tears that rooted me to the spot. My mind went blank; all I could do was sob uncontrollably.

I lost track of how much time passed. Tears clouded my vision; the world became a faded grey, like a failed watercolour. Outside the window, a deathly silence reigned. In despair, I reached to close the window. Then, at that very moment, I saw something on the deck. Though my vision was clouded with tears, I could see clearly enough: it was Pumpkin. She stood there, perfectly still, staring directly at me. For a second, I felt as if I were seeing a ghost. Had she come to say goodbye? But then, the small figure walked slowly towards me.

I snapped back to reality. *Pumpkin is alive!* Miraculously, she had returned to me. I wrenched open the screen door and welcomed her inside. She was covered by fallen leaves and smelled of earth, but I found no sign of injury. She was different, yet there was also a newfound confidence, a quiet strength in her eyes. The timid, indoor cat I knew was gone.

A cat at peace in the sanctuary of home. A cat inhaling the scent of the garden grass, freely savouring its gifts. A cat venturing into the unknown. A cat engaged in a serious struggle with other small creatures. And finally, a cat returning to the warmth of home. Each encounter with a cat is a unique, irreplaceable moment. Each cat is a precious companion, sharing this present moment with us. Each cat lives each moment to the fullest, in the place it has been given. Each cat's life holds deep meaning. Before

I knew it, I saw myself reflected in the cat's experiences. To live each moment to the fullest, wherever you are—that is what truly matters. Wherever we are, the value of life remains unchanged. Accepting both joy and sorrow, simply living—that is everything.

I decided then that I would no longer allow my wheelchair to be a prison of the mind. The gentle touch of a warm spring wind graced my cheek. The large stone in the garden stood serenely, as if the vapor it had released were a thing of the past. Its steadfast presence rekindled within me a sense of hope for what was to come, a yearning for new encounters and adventures. I am sure Pumpkin felt it too.

MEANING OF THE LAND

Nearly a month has passed since I had the difficult exchange with my father regarding the land entitlement. We have not spoken directly by phone since then. With each passing day, I sense the growing distance between us expanding further and further. It marks the first time in my life that I actively avoid speaking to him and feel fearful of inadvertently saying something that could further damage our relationship. Simultaneously, I dread the possibility of being hurt by his harsh words. Previously, I communicated with him every day through LINE with short texts and photos. Now, I fear I will lose my father while he is alive.

DID I BELONG TO THAT LAND?
watercolour, 12 × 9

Thinking of my birthplace, I wonder if it's truly the land. Perhaps we originate from the ocean and, ultimately, from the universe itself.

Initially, I sense some resistance from my father and sister regarding my plans to come to Japan with a friend or an assistant. This resistance perhaps stems from unspoken concerns about bringing non-family members into their home, a still somewhat unfamiliar concept in conventional Japanese households. However, for me to maintain my independence, it's essential. I feel it is important to discuss these options, especially about how I can maintain a connection to my childhood home, even if my visits are infrequent.

However, a more pressing issue needs to be addressed. The emotional undercurrent, the turmoil within me, is being ignored. The conversation revolves solely around the logistics of inheriting the land and building a new house. I realize my intense emotional response stems from a fear of being sidelined, my dignity disregarded because of my life abroad. Without acknowledging and validating these feelings, any progress on practical matters seems impossible.

However, for much of the month, I find myself avoiding deep reflection on my profound sense of insecurity and inexplicable psychological attachment to the land. It's all ego, I know. I withdraw from active participation in our family LINE conversations, even on mundane, everyday topics. Observing the continued activity in the family LINE between my father and my sister's family, I feel as if I have been forgotten, leaving me melancholic. Though my sister privately sends me kind messages and informs me of how our father cares about me, I feel quite depressed. "I am avoiding him. Does he avoid me, too?" I write to my sister.

She writes back, "Not at all, even I can't reach him as he is often busy with his golf and *onsen*. Don't worry."

She is probably right that I should not worry. Still, I remain unwavering in my determination to preserve my connection to the land in my hometown despite the myriad challenges posed by my own health, by the lack of accessibility in my hometown for wheelchairs, by the increasing heat caused by climate change, and even by the ever-present threat of earthquakes that the Japanese have lived with for millennia.

Confronted by a guilt-ridden conscience, I grapple with the dilemma of surrendering my land title. This inner turmoil seems akin to an existential crisis, demanding careful and swift consideration. I feel as though my father has relegated me to a less important role in managing the family house, and my ego suffers in this conflict. I acknowledge that the likelihood of my returning to live in Japan is nearly nonexistent, given the fulfillment and purpose I have found in Vancouver. It seems more and more fitting for my sister to inherit the land given that she resides in Japan and is better equipped to physically care for our father. I even seek advice from my daughter. During our video call, Maya offers a compassionate perspective, emphasizing, "Mending your relationship with your father is the most important thing."

I begin to consider the possibility that I might have to sever my ties to Japan. If I did sever my ties, I would be sharing the fate of many immigrants who, lacking land or a true home to return to, find themselves adrift. I long for the peace of Zen Buddhism, the ability to detach from material possessions and accept the world around me without the constant need to be at its centre.

Every day, the idea of reaching out to my father lingers in my thoughts with my inner voice expressing, *Father, it's okay now. I will respect your decision, whatever it may be. I should be grateful for your thoughtfulness about the whole matter.* Yet, in the next moment, waves of remorse sweep over me as I ponder, *Oh, no, it's over. There is no other place in Japan that I'd want to return to freely. And what if I want to live in Japan in my final years?*

All these thoughts emerge from hypothetical scenarios. What prompted these conflicting emotions? What is truly unfolding within me? I realize I am still viewing the situation in black and white. I recognize my reluctance to fully embrace my immigrant status, unwilling to let go of the pride and privileges of being a Japanese citizen. Is it covetousness? Perhaps an unconscious sibling rivalry? Or simply a lack of courage? Whatever the reason, I remain uncertain about the root cause behind my inability to let go.

One day, my sister texts me asking me to call her as soon as possible as she needs to convey a message from our father. I tell her that I will get in touch after my upcoming public speaking event. The truth is, I need to gather all my positive energy to ensure a successful delivery. I anticipate our father's message to be a final, unwelcome decision. Is this merely another excuse of mine to delay the difficult conversation? Nonetheless, staying true to my word, I call her shortly after my talk.

My sister appears unchanged, wearing, as always, a caring smile. After some casual conversation, she shares our father's proposal, noting, "He dedicated a significant amount of time considering things from your perspective and how he could fulfill your wishes." I swallowed nervously as she adds: "He has decided to buy our grandparents' house and land, which still has shared land entitlement among all our cousins and so poses complications. Despite his previous belief that the grandparents' house and land should go to our late mother's eldest brother's family, he is now willing to buy it out and give it to you if the rest of our families agreed. This way, you can have a piece of land that holds the deepest connection for you." As I am the only cousin born in our grandparents' home and affectionately raised by them, their house holds my truest origins, brimming with cherished memories.

I am taken aback; my eyes are filled with tears. I am astonished that my father would make such a bold and unexpected decision merely to accommodate my selfish desire. Previously he has been uninvolved in matters concerning our mother's side of the family, and he always supported her adherence to the patriarchal system. His change of stance indicates he gave considerable thought to his proposal.

"What are your thoughts, Keiko? Our father will only proceed if you are content with his decision. I will help facilitate this process by reaching out to all our cousins. I'm confident there will be no objections if you take charge," my sister says, adding, "Our father's intention is to effectively and meaningfully use his resources while considering what's best for you. He deeply cares about your welfare."

"Hmm, I must admit I'm quite surprised because I never considered that option. However, I am deeply grateful for our father's thoughtfulness, creative thinking, and sacrifice, knowing that buying out is expensive. While I would love to transform our grandparents' home to honour our cultural family heritage, perhaps as a small art gallery or something similar, I also sense a deep responsibility," I reply, expressing, I hope, both excitement and caution.

After that conversation, a spectrum of possibilities fills my mind. I realize I have underestimated my father's capabilities. His willingness to alter his stance and propose such a bold idea has caught me off guard. Yet, alongside this surprise, I feel a pang of selfishness. It dawns on me that my ego has intertwined the land with my identity. Am I unwittingly stirring up trouble? Or am I evolving into a legacy-maker for our family? Unsure of the answer, my perspective broadens, as if beams of light are breaking through.

For the next few days, I ponder the new horizon with a mix of emotions. I can't quite grasp my own feelings. After all, this is something I have long wished for and now, with my father's endorsement and assistance, it is within reach. So why do I not feel as compelled as I anticipated? Over dinner, I discuss the matter with my girlfriend. She is another middle-aged, single immigrant from Asia. She shares that she has no desire to inherit her mother's property as she knows she will never live there. Instead, she envisions prioritizing freedom in retirement over taking on additional responsibilities. I ask about her sense of identity, particularly regarding the impact of losing the physical connection to her homeland. She smiles and replies, "I am a Canadian now." This leaves a lasting impression on me with her blend of traditional Asian humility and grace.

I also talk about the issue with Maya. She listens patiently while I ask, "Maya, what are your thoughts? I understand you may not have any emotional attachment to my grandparents' home."

She responds frankly, "I don't really care, Mom. It's up to you."

Her response, though seemingly indifferent, forces me to look at the situation with fresh eyes. I thank her for her honesty and then jot down new insights.

A week later, I try to call my father to thank him, but he is unavailable. Instead, I write a long text to him: "Dear Father, I trust this message finds you in good health. I want to express my sincere gratitude for your thoughtfulness. After much contemplation, I've made the decision not to inherit either your land or my grandparents' land. I also discussed this matter with Maya. My primary reason for this choice is to avoid any complications for her, as she has no interest in inheriting land in Japan. Additionally, I came to realize that I had misunderstood my identity and purpose. Recognizing the deep bond I share with you and our family, my attachment to material possessions dissolved. You are right; home resides within our hearts. Moreover, I've come to understand that my life's purpose lies in living fully and leaving a legacy through my skills and sensibilities, rather than through property ownership. While I do miss my home and our family in Japan dearly, and this longing has only grown with age, I want to thank you for instilling in me trust, love, and courage. I eagerly anticipate our future conversations. Please take good care of yourself."

I feel a profound sense of unity, as if I have finally reconciled my divided self and found a sense of belonging where I currently live. Shortly after, my friend Gail Sparrow, former Musqueam Chief, stops by to pick up the green tea that my sister sent from my hometown in Japan. I share with her my recent experiences and realizations about land entitlement. She listens attentively and then smiles, saying, "Keiko, you're here now. You're standing on this land. It's yours." At this, she gently taps the ground beneath her feet. With a newfound sense of empowerment, I embrace my immigrant identity wholeheartedly. Ultimately, I realize that I belong to the earth, a shared home for all.

THE WAY WE MOVE

My girlfriend has also recently entered the empty-nest phase and is living independently. She asks me how I maintain a consistently positive mindset and how I stay productive amid life challenges, aging, and vulnerability. Her question strikes a chord with me. I wonder how several successful male colleagues—divorcees and single parents of grown-up kids—skillfully balance professional responsibilities with personal pursuits as they age. Curious, I had asked them how they stay energized and

THE WAY WE MOVE
watercolour, 9 × 12

The orchid, given to me by a friend, is in full bloom, radiating vibrant life. It seems to be examining itself carefully from all angles, left, right, up, and down. It stands like a noble lady, dignified and upright, as if aware of its own beauty.

content while remaining unattached. Interestingly, my male friends admitted to missing intimacy and female energy but said they prioritize their independence and freedom. I laughingly suggested, "Perhaps we are alike!" Now, I wonder whether these desires are truly gender specific.

"Hmmm, it may have something to do with my character," I say to my girlfriend. "I always crave something new and easily get excited." Even as I say it, I feel that my answer is not well thought out, and her question stays with me.

My grandmother, Tamiko, comes to mind. It isn't just that she was consistently calm and affectionate; she was also diligent and hardworking, traits I've always admired. Even in moments when my mother chided her for missing medicine or spoiling her granddaughters, her signature phrase, *arigatou gozaimasu* (thank you in an honorific way), accompanied by her gentle smile and a graceful bow, brought laughter and joy to the room. Her every movement and gesture flowed like a dance. I recall how she would rise and then sit again at the low-rise Japanese table during mealtimes to serve others, all while moving with precise graceful movement, as if she wore a kimono. Her posture remained impeccably straight. In Japanese, we have a word for this, *sho-sa* (所作), signifying the way one carries oneself. Even in my childhood, her graceful demeanour stood out in our family. As I grow older, I long to emulate her conduct, but find it challenging to replicate, particularly during moments of frustration.

Now in my fifties, I'm contemplating the connection between internal spiritual states and external appearances. Facial expressions can display thought patterns, the state of our hearts, and our values. My grandmother's countenance always radiated a vibrant warmth, and she embodied spirituality through her daily Buddhist practices. Each morning, she'd offer prayers, present fresh white rice and green tea to our ancestors, light incense, and meticulously tend to the altar's flowers by refreshing their water.

Living a life is itself a form of art. To emulate my grandmother's grace, I must cultivate her inner spirituality—like an artist seeking inspiration. An artist's thoughts create form. For example, take Paul Cezanne, my favourite painter, and consider his intricate watercolour and pencil renderings of rocks near the caves above Château Noir in Aix-en-Provence. I love how these detailed and vibrant pieces straddle representation and abstraction while still depicting recognizable landscapes. Those airy, colourful rocks, arising from Cezanne's inner state, resonate with my own mental landscape. My grandmother exuded deep happiness because she naturally nurtured these qualities through her *sho-sa,* evoking a warm happiness in those around her.

Emulating my grandmother's demeanour and smiles, along with the thoughts that gave rise to them, I am extending gratitude, *arigatō*, to everything around me, including my own body. I appreciate my resilient heart and even my imperfect toenails, despite the troubles they sometimes cause. I redefine my daily rituals, such as showering, transforming them into a choreographed art form reminiscent of the tea ceremonies I once studied, rather than mere washing up. Previously, when feeling fatigued, showering felt like a chore, demanding precise effort and balance in shifting between my chair and the shower bench. Over time, I begin noticing a heightened sense of grace and aesthetic joy.

Reflecting on my girlfriend's question, I am coming to realize that my true answer lies within this everyday *sho-sa*, a practice instilled in me by my grandmother. While perfection remains unattainable, simple happiness does not require perfection.

PERFECT DAYS

At the 2024 Vancouver International Film Festival, I attend a screening of *Perfect Days*, directed by Wim Wenders. Although I haven't watched any of his films before, I am aware of this one. It features the Japanese actor Kōji Yakusho, who won the Best Actor Award at the 2023 Cannes Film Festival for his role in the film.

The theatre is bustling with people taking advantage of the $5 Movie Tuesday promotion. It is so crowded that even my wheelchair companion seat is made available for sale. With much anticipation, the film starts.

It isn't until later that I realize there isn't much dialogue in the film. Despite this, I soon feel as though I am merging with the main character, Mr. Hirayama (literally meaning "peaceful mountain"), a public toilet cleaner living a solitary life and skillfully portrayed by Kōji Yakusho. In the film, Mr. Hirayama adheres to his everyday routines without much human interaction. He reads books, tends to houseplants, cleans public toilets for work, and observes *komorebi*, the sunlight filtering through trees. The film moves slowly and subtly yet is so visceral that I feel my five senses meld with those of Mr. Hirayama. In fact, throughout the entire film, I am simply experiencing, without actively engaging in thought, and my senses seem to sharpen as the story progresses. Afterward, I reflect on the experience. I feel transformed, my senses open, my thoughts fleeting—as if in a Zen-like state. A sense of joy and serenity lingers long after the credits have rolled.

Straight after watching the film, I contact my family in Japan, urging them to watch the film. I especially encourage my closest cousin Toshio to go see it. We grew up together in our hometown, and he's always been like a brother to me. Toshio is not only handsome but also kind, intelligent, and deeply sensitive, qualities that have always made him beloved by everyone who knows him. Aside from navigating the challenges of divorce, much like I did, he has generally enjoyed a relatively smooth life. With a BA in literature, he pursued his passion and became a Japanese literature teacher at a junior high school. It's been eighteen years since our last meeting, during my trip to Japan in 2006, yet our bond has only grown stronger despite the distance. Even though he's nearing age forty-six, I still call him "Toshi-bō," the same nickname I used when he was a baby, and he affectionately calls me "Keiko-chan" in return.

ME: Toshi-bō, how was the film? Did Hirayama's presence resonate with you? It made me think about the nature of happiness. It seems we can't truly live unless we engage our senses, rather than just thinking. It's almost Zen-like. Hirayama's life echoes our grandparents' lives in some ways—that living with a pure heart, that broad perspective. I'm far from that, but I aspire to find joy in the everyday. Looking forward to your thoughts!

Toshio immediately sends me a photo of the five bonsai trees in his garden. Bonsai is the Japanese art of growing and shaping miniature trees in containers. Each tree, meticulously shaped and pruned, speaks of patience and care, a connection to nature distilled into art.

TOSHIO: Mr. Hirayama and I share a hobby! The apple tree and cherry blossom are about to bloom. Thanks for the movie, Keiko-chan! It was great to watch one again. I loved the music and Tokyo scenery. But I noticed Hirayama eating a sandwich after cleaning toilets, hanging work clothes unwashed, and slamming loud car/house doors. Am I too picky? I guess I need to learn more. I feel happy to be alive, have meaningful work, and meet interesting people. Is that aging? I've been thinking about light and shadow. What's the meaning of *komorebi* in the credits? What did Hirayama mean about overlapping shadows? What do you think, Keiko-chan?

ME: Your bonsai is truly wonderful, Toshi-bō. It evokes Mr. Hirayama so perfectly! And it tickled me to discover that we both shared the same slight irritation at the scene with the unwashed work clothes. It seems we have similar sensibilities! The shadow-stepping scene also resonated with me. I think Mr. Hirayama's ability to simply say "let's give it a try" stems from his deep connection to lived experience, rather than just intellectualizing. Most people might dismiss such an idea as unimportant, or perhaps even over analyze it. *Komorebi* is such a beautiful word, isn't it? Like *yūgen* and *ikigai*, it's a concept so uniquely Japanese that it often fascinates those from other cultures. These nuanced sensitivities and expressions are such treasures of our culture. I don't know if it's simply a matter of age, but your gentle nature and profound insights feel so innate, Toshi-bō. Your current profession truly seems to be your calling! All that's left is for you to write a novel, and you'll have achieved perfection! On the subject of music, what are you currently enjoying?

TOSHIO: I suppose it's an occupational hazard, isn't it? I tend to overanalyze the nuances of language, the motivations behind actions, and the subtle details of landscape descriptions. For example, I've been pondering whether

Mr. Hirayama finds a particular beauty in shadows that surpasses his appreciation of light. As you so aptly pointed out, the word *komorebi* itself encapsulates a uniquely Japanese sensibility. As for my current musical inclinations, I find myself drawn to a lot of instrumental pieces these days. Solo piano music, particularly from the classical and jazz genres, has been a constant companion. When there are lyrics, I tend to focus on them intently. Perhaps it's an artist's tendency to be drawn to narrative.

ME: Shadows are fascinating; so many interpretations! That dream scene felt like reality—formless, changing, intangible. It would be great to accept it as it is and find the beauty. Guess who was in Vancouver today? Keiichiro Hirano! I couldn't miss the chance to hear him speak—the Akutagawa Prize winner! I loved his idea of "discovering oneself" while writing. I even had the chance to give him a copy of my memoir as I left.

TOSHIO: I'm rereading recent Akutagawa Prize winners. I'll check out Hirano's book too. Your dream interpretation was great! One last thing—the leaf-sweeping sound in the morning reminded me so much of our Grandma Tamiko. And I love how it connected the dream and real life. Thanks for the great movie rec!

We conclude our LINE chat for the day. The following afternoon, I find myself in the kitchen. Warm afternoon sunlight streams in from the west window, casting rays that dance across the room. I notice the cedar foliage outside swaying in the wind, the cast shadows painting patterns on the kitchen wall opposite the window. It reminds me of the dreamlike shadow scenes from *Perfect Days*—layers of soft shadows moving in and out of view. Toshio's question pops into my mind: "What did Mr. Hirayama mean when he insisted that shadows become denser when they overlap, as depicted in the scene where two adult men step on shadows?" Curious, I continue to gaze at the mesmerizing display on my kitchen wall. I observe how the shapeless shadows indeed grow denser as they overlap. I grab my iPhone and capture the scene and send it straight to Toshio.

ME: As I happened to see this shadow just now, I recalled Toshi-bō's question about shadows and the scene where Hirayama emphasized that when shadows overlap during shadow-stepping, they become darker. Actually, I had overlooked that part before. But now, interpreting it, I wonder if it is meant to convey the idea that while individuals may be weak on their own, they can become stronger through helping each other?

TOSHIO: I loved your idea about "helping each other" and light and shadows. Hirayama seems alone, but he has so many people who care about him—his coworkers, the diner people, the snack bar lady, his family. They're not like bright lights, but maybe they're like those overlapping shadows, you know? With *komorebi* I always think of the light, but it's really the shadows that make it so nice. And shadows need light, but maybe we need those "shadow people" too. Maybe Hirayama wanted to be that for someone. His sister probably wanted to be in the spotlight, but sometimes it's too much, like the summer sun. Maybe that's why her daughter ran to her uncle. Anyway, that's what I got from the light and shadow in the movie. That concludes my analysis of the film. Ah, it's so fascinating!

ME: Your writing is so readable, with a lovely rhythm. You are a pro! I love your "It is fascinating!" I can feel your joy. Expressing ourselves is an art, isn't it? Your insights are so profound, as expected from a literature teacher. The sister/niece analogy—the scorching sun versus dappled light—really struck me. It made me think about my relationship with Maya. We all want that "dappled sunlight" feeling, don't we? This movie is a thought-provoking experience, best enjoyed when you bring your own questions to it. I'd love to discuss books and movies with you sometime.

After sending the message, I rush to my desk and jot down seemingly unrelated ideas that, I hope, might one day converge. The term "grey" I used in my message to Toshio dovetails with the concept of greyscale, which I often reference in conversations and that serves as an analogy for co-creation with my colleagues.

As I mentioned before, greyscale draws from the concept of dynamic range and refers to a spectrum of shades from pure white to pure black with various gradations in between. It represents the diverse levels of brightness or luminance within an image or visual display.

In photography, it plays a vital role in depicting the full range of tones and contrasts, allowing for the accurate rendering of highlights, mid-tones, and shadows, thus preserving the intricate details and nuances within different areas of the image.

The concept of greyscale, of a suspension between black and white, mirrors the Zen Buddhist notion of *Mu*—a dynamic, fertile emptiness that transcends duality. Watching the foliage sway, I feel that *Mu*, that oneness with nature that Hirayama experiences in *Perfect Days*. It is wonder, humility, gentleness, and joy. The light and shadow on the foliage reveal hidden depths, as did my conversations with Toshio. Our talks explore our experiences and perspectives, acknowledging we can be "shadow people."

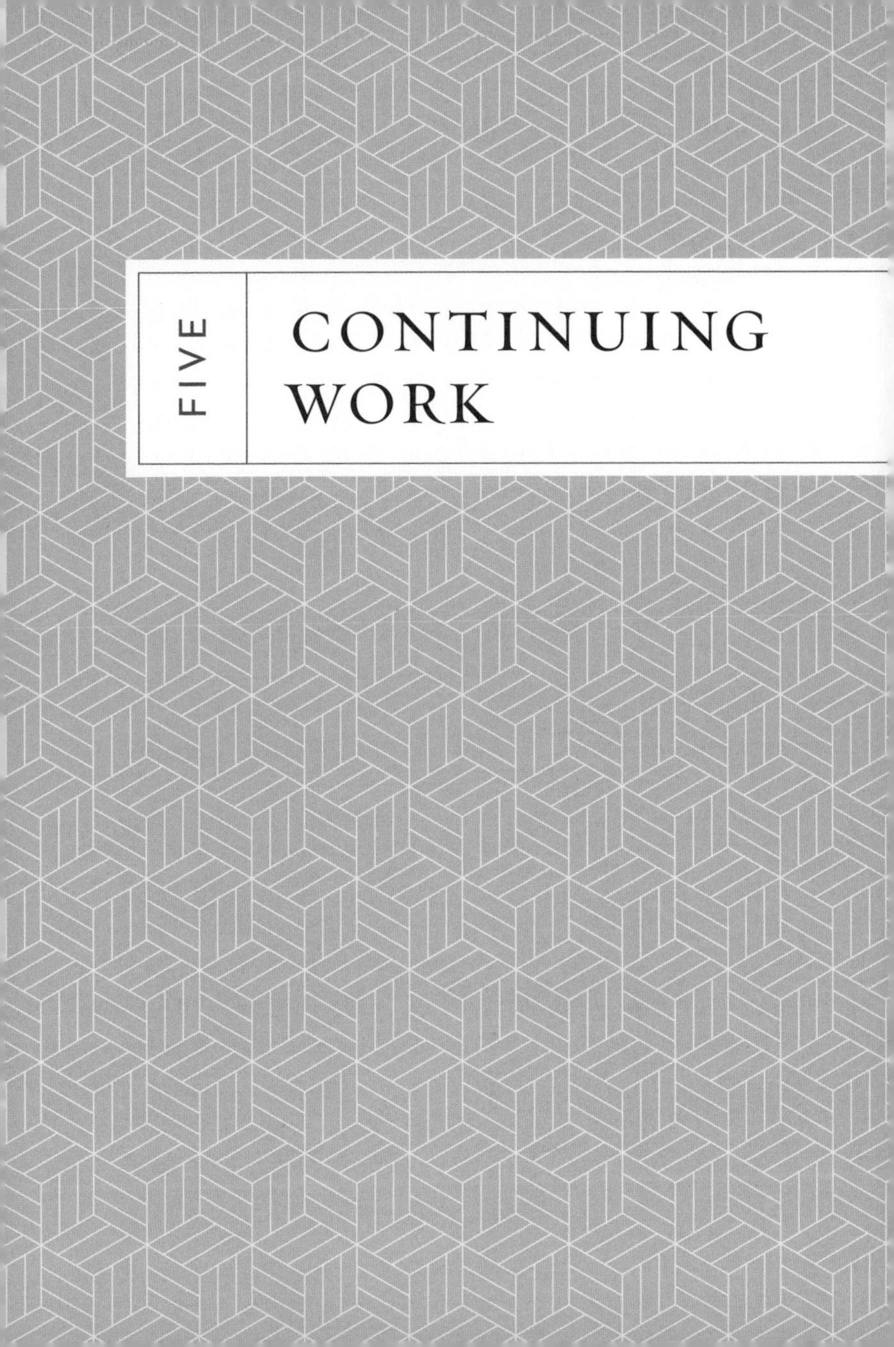

FIVE

CONTINUING WORK

AWAITING
watercolour,
12 × 9

On my desk, a scatter of paint tubes lies in wait, anticipating the touch of my brushes. They seem almost eager. I imagine them whispering to each other, "When will she begin?"

住する所なきを、まず花と知るべし。

One should know that something with no permanent abode is, first and foremost, like a flower.

ZEAMI MOTOKIYO

NOH MASTER ZEAMI once profoundly mentioned that constant change without stagnation is the centre of the art. As the founder and director of a non-profit, this strikes me deeply. The temptation to seek stability is ever-present. Yet I understand that true vitality lies in continuous innovation, in forging new connections, and in embracing the ever-changing landscape. Just as a flower blooms, fades, and then gives way to new life, I must constantly evolve to remain vital to my surroundings.

This need for adaptability is echoed in anthropologist Claude Lévi-Strauss's description of the *bricoleur* in his book, *The Savage Mind*. The *bricoleur*, unlike the engineer, doesn't plan for specific materials; instead, they skillfully utilize "whatever is at hand," working within a "closed universe of instruments." This resourceful approach, this ability to create something new from existing resources, is essential for navigating the ever-changing world of a non-profit, constantly adapting to new challenges and opportunities.

REVOLVING DANCE

On a quiet autumn afternoon after Maya's departure, I welcome the solitude of my empty house. I keenly observe the movements of my body: my weary eyes, my stiff neck, my resilient shoulders, my atrophied spinal muscles, my still flexible pelvis, and my chilly toes. I am struck by my body's smooth, almost choreographed movements, like a Calder mobile that floats and turns with the slightest touch.

What will I explore in this new phase? Will I continue to blossom? As I sit, a stillness creeps in, a warning against stagnation. I must embrace movement. I dance with time, resisting and accepting. I chase fleeting moments through writing; yet time won't wait; it is indifferent to my desires. The elusive key, I suspect, lies in the delicate art of balancing these opposing forces within me.

Lately, I've been experiencing persistent tension, mostly concentrated in my back. I see this as a warning sign that I am falling back into workaholic patterns and ignoring my body's signals. I start thinking about the exercise routines of my friends who are close to my age. I remember Shu's daily breathing routine, visualizing him stepping out of his office onto an outdoor terrace to engage in meditative or martial arts–like movements, and all without caring about onlookers. My friend Aimee heads to the ocean before dawn to swim gracefully with other ladies in the therapeutic ice-cold waters. My high school friend Tomo, despite his busy academic career, maintains a running regimen and even runs marathons. Their lifestyles demonstrate that a sound mind thrives within a healthy body and underscores the importance of nurturing well-being from a young age. They even offer me a sample of their routines and encourage me to join them.

In the past, I've experimented with various adaptive exercise options, such as enrolling in online wheelchair yoga and stretching classes and visiting the iCord gym, a facility dedicated to advancing research on exercise and physical activity for people with spinal cord injuries. However, the only endeavour that has endured is my use of a standing desk at home, and even this I only use a few times a week.

I realize I need to find my own wheelchair dance. At home, I begin with simple movements, gently swaying my torso, grounding myself in the moment. Slowly, I'm adding more movements—a twist of the shoulders, a lift of an arm. It's becoming more than just movement; it's becoming *my* dance.

MEANING OF OUR LIVES

Meaning of Our Lives is the title of our new documentary, a project created together with youthful collaborators during the summer of 2023. We considered numerous titles but ultimately chose this one.

My goal with the documentary was to weave a collective narrative for our weaving group, aptly named Weaving Our Way (WOW). I originally launched this project through my non-profit organization that was funded by a City of Vancouver Community Arts grant in 2016. Since then, we have blossomed into a thriving, self-sustaining group. This group is truly exceptional, characterized by creativity, friendship, and peer mentoring. I set out to discover a theme or approach that would encompass all the subtleties and intricacies that we, as a group, have yet to convey.

The elusiveness of both nature and *wabi-sabi*—the Japanese aesthetic of imperfection and impermanence—fascinates me. Japan's diverse ecosystem, born of its unique geography and climate, perfectly embodies this elusive beauty. From its varied forests and abundant species to the rich marine life brought forth by the influence of eight major ocean currents, the country reflects a complex, interconnected harmony, much of which remains unseen. The Japanese people, it seems, have long recognized their connection to this intricate web. *Wabi-sabi* feels like a cultural expression of this very elusiveness, a wisdom that defies easy categorization. Is this appreciation part of my Japanese heritage, or is it a more personal connection? I wonder how these cultural currents have shaped WOW.

My eighty-seven-year-old father made a remarkable solo trip from Japan to see me, bringing with him my mother's ashes. They were held in the simple cypress urn we had chosen after the emotional conflict surrounding the tea canister—a disagreement that now feels like a lifetime ago. He quietly passed the urn to me. Together, we placed it next to the miniature Zen garden I had arranged in anticipation of this moment: the smooth white sand, the carefully selected rocks, the miniature raking tools—a small sanctuary of peace.

Now as I carefully rake the white sand, I'm transported to Ryōan-ji Temple in Kyoto, imagining myself among the monks who have tended its celebrated fifteenth-century rock garden for generations. Instead of using rocks, I decide to use my collection of seashells to mimic islands in the ocean. I place a white clamshell on the wave-patterned white sand and then rake again around it, just as the monks at Ryōan-ji do. The result is astonishing; it truly resembles an island in the ocean. The process carries me away, and it feels remarkably appropriate to honour my mother's urn in this manner. In that small rectangular tray, the entire universe seems to come to life.

I have a deep fascination for seashells; they are like works of art. It's incredible how slugs and snails can craft such a diverse array of shells from their own bodies, each shell possessing its own unique shape, colour, and texture. This intricate process reminds me of my mother, who, in her own way, expressed her personality throughout the different phases of her life.

I chuckle as I recall her distinctive clothing choices, which evolved over the years: the combination of jeans and a denim vest in her thirties and forties; the pairing of black spats and a short black skirt in her fifties; her elegant choices from the Shisendo brand made of kimono fabric in her sixties; and her preference for sporty and functional

Japanese brands like Adabat in her seventies. She also had an extensive collection of hats, never leaving home without one. Her own father was the same and he never left home without his signature bucket hat. Each phase of her life came with a unique mode of exterior self-expression, much like the seashells I admire.

But there's a poetic aspect to it: when those slugs pass away, their shells break down into small pieces against the rocks, eventually becoming soft sand that blends with countless other grains. It's a natural cycle that makes me ponder our own life journey.

When I rake the white sand, I feel like I am connecting with the wisdom of my ancestors, with my beloved grandparents, uncles, and mother, and perhaps even with people I never knew. I wonder about my own life, too. One day, I will join the sand and become part of something greater by leaving some intangible legacy, much like those shells eventually become one with the sand.

As I continue tending to the miniature Zen garden, my fingers delicately tracing the patterns in the white sands, I realize that the intricate life cycle of seashells beautifully mirrors the essence of the documentary project I have been diligently working on with the weaving group. Initially, the project was a journey of self-discovery for the group and ventured deeply into the intricate world of weaving, culture, and personal narratives. But soon, the theme of transience and the motif of seashells merged with other thematic threads. I had been exploring the interconnectedness of life, the threads that bind us together, and the intricate tapestry we weave as individuals in our diverse and complex society. These themes are captured by the hidden stories of the seashells I admire.

Like the creatures within, each member of our WOW group carries a unique history, a tapestry of experiences that, like the seashells, can tell individual tales. Yet, just like the shells' eventual journey to become part of the shoreline, we, too, will reach the ends of our individual paths, blending into something greater. Each of our stories and weavings will merge with the collective experiences of our group, making a broader narrative.

In that small Zen garden, the interconnectedness of our lives becomes vividly clear. I feel this insight will infuse our documentary with the intimate dance between individuality and collective experience, a theme that resonates deeply with all of us.

SPACE(S)

The Dunbar Community Centre approaches me to screen *Meanings of Our Lives.* This is during the week of the National Day for Truth and Reconciliation. As the day of the premiere finally arrives, I feel that some entity with a kind heart must be watching over us.

Creating art is labour intensive enough; but promoting and sharing it with the community adds another layer of complexity, especially if you aren't well known. The initiative for the screening came from Kristi, the recreation

MOSS-COVERED ROCKS
watercolour, 12 × 9

Moss-covered rocks are a cornerstone of Japanese aesthetics, emphasizing the beauty of relational continuity that emerges over time. My Japanese rock garden, through its gradual transformation, has become a living embodiment of this profound wisdom.

supervisor of the centre, with whom I had collaborated a decade ago. Separately, I am also approached by a young student, Isabel, the director of UBC's student-run Hatch Gallery, to collaborate on their upcoming exhibition, titled *Space(s)*. Interestingly, this opportunity arose through Michael, the facility manager of the UBC Alma Mater Society, with whom I had collaborated on our first weaving exhibition back in 2017. I don't know what to call these delightful connections from the past, but it certainly seems that everything is interconnected.

During the screening, I take pleasure in the reactions of the audience, their hushed whispers, appreciative sighs, or bursts of laughter. They appear to immerse themselves in the world of creative weaving and the sense of community and bonding depicted in the film. After the screening, they erupt in applause. A woman approaches me and, gazing into my eyes, says, "You're a catalyst. You know that, right? You've changed our community." Others told me they could feel the love and trust the weavers had for me in the way they so freely shared their authentic voices. The event attracts many new community members eager to join the weaving group. What more could I ask for!

The title of the upcoming group exhibition at UBC's Hatch Gallery, *Space{s}*, has been haunting my thoughts. I'm fascinated by the different kinds of spaces that shape us—from the microscopic space of our DNA to the expansive space of our beginnings. For weavers, the double-stranded warp (the vertical threads that are held taut on a loom *before* the weaving process begins) creates a unique kind of foundational space, a framework within which we deliberately weave stories and meaning, much like the intricate code of our DNA. The warp represents a field of potential, its final form yet to be revealed. With each pass of the horizontal weft, each "filling" thread, we begin to weave our thoughts, emotions, and dreams into existence. This foundation is both the starting point and the key to the entire process.

Communal spaces, though often undervalued, are vital to our well-being. Yet, in these times of a relentless housing crisis and a market-driven economy that prioritizes profit over people, free communal spaces are vanishing. Where can we find these essential safe havens?

As I contemplate this, it becomes increasingly evident how this screening clarifies our need for communal spaces where we can evolve together. Remarkably, the storytelling weavers featured in our film come from all over the world, including South Africa, France, the Netherlands, Australia, Japan, Musqueam, and more. Each woman carries with her the memories of her homeland and a unique perspective that she artfully expresses through her woven blankets. These blankets themselves become shared spaces where the seemingly disparate forces of individuality and community come together in harmonious expression.

Furthermore, these blankets enable these women to reimagine themselves beyond society's preconceived notions concerning liveliness and attractiveness. These women have boundless sensibility, imagination, and creativity, and they defy the ageist stereotypes that may hold them back. An older couple from the audience speaks, as if on cue: "It's so wonderful to see older women featured in films and to see their beauty and resilience, as they're so underrepresented."

"Yes!" I agree. "And it is important for men, too, to see older women thriving."

Whether the audience fully grasps my original intention of interweaving the life cycle of seashells with our own creative journey remains uncertain, but I sense that they appreciate the ever-evolving nature of identity and community.

The magic of that re-perception lies in the moment we recognize the potential in a seemingly empty space. It is much like a blank canvas awaiting its first brushstroke or a weaving loom ready to be threaded. Empty nesting? Let's call it something else.

THE SHELLF

The day of the opening of the exhibition, *Space(s)* finally arrives, January 18. More snow falls than anticipated, and freezing temperatures bring public transportation to a near standstill. It is *Daikan* (大寒), the coldest period of the year according to the traditional Japanese calendar. Yet, a reminder from our elders echoes in my mind: beneath the surface, nature is already preparing for the rebirth of spring. Collaborating with young students feels like a harbinger of spring. Six members of our group—Jill, Gail, Saskia, Josette, Barb, and CZarina—present their distinct woven creations, comprising a total of fifty-three pieces. Other dedicated members, including Carla and some spouses, Mark and Maarten, generously offer their help the week before to set up the show. It is a real team effort.

I name our exhibition *The Shellf*, a word combining "shell" and "self," to symbolize how the small reflects the large. While giving a short speech, I hold a large seashell and explain how seashells represent our weaving exhibit, and how they are also metaphors for the spaces we create. I emphasize that, like seashells, we each create our

大寒 **(DAIKAN)**
watercolour,
11 × 8

The morning of *Daikan* dawns, and the sound, "chun-chun," fills the air outside my bathroom window. It must be black-capped chickadees and Pacific wrens, their cheerful calls a testament to life's resilience. Though the temperature plummets, these tiny creatures persist, adapting to the harshest conditions. Their voices, so small yet so powerful, fill my heart with awe.

own unique spaces through incremental growth. Just as no two shells are alike, neither are we. Our weavings, like seashells, show this beautiful diversity while sharing a common foundation: the warp threads. To illustrate how our creations, even if they change or disappear, contribute to something larger—like seashells becoming sand—we even created a small sand garden at the corner for contemplation, inviting the audience to reflect on the spaces they will create and that will perhaps become a legacy for future generations.

"Our exhibition," I continue, "is more than a display of weavings; it's a journey into poetry, philosophy, and the human drive to explore the unknown. So, take a moment to enjoy the diverse expressions of our talented weavers. Their creativity and identity are magically woven into each piece through their hands, much like sea snails expressing something from within to fashion their unique homes. Then it's your turn to imagine your own expressions."

At the end of our presentation, Jill, our ninety-year-old inspiration, the oldest member of our group, speaks to the audience, a twinkle in her eye. "For all you young people here," she says, her voice strong and clear, "find a hobby, something you love, and keep doing it all your life." Such simple yet profound wisdom. That's what life's all about.

HIDDEN FLOWERS PROJECT

My debut memoir recounts a moment of delightful surprise and kindness from a friend, a moment I still cherish, echoing the wisdom of Zeami's *Fushikaden*: "When it is hidden, it is the flower." The profound philosophy behind this quote, the notion of hidden flowers, continues to intrigue me.

COMMUNITIES OF PRACTICE
watercolour, 8 × 11

A dear friend, a true lover of nature, always arrives at my door bearing a fragrant bouquet freshly plucked from her garden. Each unique arrangement is a testament to her artistry and reminds me of the diverse yet harmonious way my like-minded friends come together to form a supportive community.

In my non-profit's newsletter dated May 2023, I wrote:

As May approaches, VACS is excited to announce our upcoming project, *Hidden Flowers*. This project draws inspiration from Zeami's philosophy on the concept of hidden flowers. While the meaning of hidden flowers can be multifaceted, Zeami views them as something new and exciting. In the world of Noh theatre, the beauty of performance is conveyed through subtle gestures and nuances that convey deeper meanings. Zeami suggests that building a strong relationship with our audience and gaining influence over them entails keen observation and thoughtful consideration to determine the optimal timing for our actions.

The beauty of grass flowers, like the Sideoats grama pictured above, captivates me. Upon closer examination, we discover a hidden world of flowering plant diversity. These flowers use wind for pollination, and their intricate perianth structure plays a crucial role in protecting the flower buds and directing pollinators toward the reproductive organs. The idea of having our own hidden flowers, or perianths, which interact with our surroundings, whether through social networks or personal rituals, is captivating to ponder.

The concept of hidden flowers within grass flowers has prompted me to contemplate the significance of creativity and how it can aid in our own personal development and in that of others. This project aims to invite both young and old to explore topics such as

> well-being, mentoring, human flourishing, and quality of social connection through creative means...

My new project seeks to celebrate the often-unseen beauty and excitement in the lives of middle-aged and older adults, including myself. It's a call to action, an invitation to appreciate the subtle intricacies and nuances that enrich and give meaning to life, requiring a dedicated effort to explore these often-overlooked aspects.

ONCE AGAIN, earlier this year, I had the privilege of teaching the course Social Artistry Through Co-Creation at SFU Continuing Studies. Before I was waiting for the class to start, a well-dressed woman with blond hair approached me.

"Hi, Keiko, do you remember me? It's Ela. We met at your film premiere of *Emerging Ancestors* two months ago!"

"Oh, yes! Wow! So..."

"Yes, I decided to take your course!"

The memory clicked. Ela! I recalled meeting her at the Roundhouse Community Arts Centre. She'd attended the premiere I hosted for *Emerging Ancestors*, a film I produced and directed. Her partner, Daniel, had apparently given her the tickets as a fiftieth birthday present—so thoughtful! At fifty, Ela was a successful corporate lawyer, yet she was at a point in her life where she was re-evaluating her purpose and direction.

After the class, she suggested meeting the following week for tea and brainstorming, expressing immense gratitude and a desire to "repay some good karma." Then she quipped that we must have met in a past life. Since then, I've become close friends with her, as well as with her husband Daniel, and we often share deep questions and personal stories over Ela's exquisite home dishes. By the end of the course, she had made a profound decision: she left her job and was excited to explore new possibilities.

Reflecting on our serendipitous connection, I wonder: What is it that draws two people together, sometimes seemingly by chance to create a bond that resonates so deeply? Is it shared values? A recognition of kindred spirits? Or something more mysterious? And how do these friendships, these unexpected gifts, shape us, challenge us, and ultimately help us to grow? I wonder about my own role in Ela's journey, and in the journeys of others like her. Am I a catalyst, a facilitator of connection? Or simply a fellow traveller? Is there something more I can do to support those who are seeking transformation? Perhaps the act of creating art, of sharing stories like *Emerging Ancestors*, is itself a form of nurturing, a way of planting seeds that may blossom in unexpected ways.

While I mull over the concept of Communities of Practice, my students seize the opportunity to establish a group they dub "CCS," an abbreviation for Continuing Continuing Studies, upon completing my course. They want to extend support to each other and actively shape their lives, rather than rely on chance. I join the group, and we decide to convene on the last Thursday of each month, creating a space for continual exchange devoid of fixed agendas or predefined objectives. I pinch myself; as an educator, this is truly the most gratifying learning outcome. Learning is one thing; translating it into action is another.

THROUGHOUT THE SUMMER of 2023 and beyond, the CCS group remains actively engaged, forging connections beyond our monthly meetings. One of our exciting endeavours is to participate in the documentary film project titled the *Hidden Flowers Project,* which I am producing and directing through my non-profit organizations. Two youth filmmakers, Harry and SiMing, collaborate with me on this project.

Creating a documentary film about the newly formed group, while simultaneously being an active member of that group, has been both challenging and exhilarating. I've had to keep both my mind and heart attuned to even the subtlest developments, both within the group dynamic and in my own evolving perspective. This constant reflection-in-action often feels like a deeply intuitive process, a dance between observation and participation.

During this second gathering of the CCS, a certain structure is beginning to take shape, with everyone eagerly anticipating their turn as both presenter and participant. Today, it is Lucy's moment to share her idea for an intergenerational paper-weaving project. Lucy, a seventy-year-old Colombian woman, has dedicated herself to education, particularly through an after-school program for school children in Vancouver. She holds a deep passion for uniting seniors and youth through art, although she has yet to fully realize her dream.

Lucy comes well prepared, not only with her speech and instructions but also with all the necessary materials neatly displayed in the room, thus creating a palpable sense of anticipation. As soon as she concludes her instructions, everyone enthusiastically dives into the creative process. I bring along a printed copy of the foreword from my upcoming memoir, intending to incorporate it somehow into the coloured paper through the weaving.

While waiting for a paper cutter to create strips, I make a spontaneous decision to tear the foreword paper with my fingers to create organic and irregular shapes. A moment of hesitancy arises—a feeling of dismantling something I have worked hard to build and perfect. Yet, almost immediately, a powerful sense of liberation follows. It is time to begin anew.

From that point on, my fingers seem to move instinctively, guided by the creative flow. As the weaving nears completion, the concept of *wabi-sabi* comes to mind. I envision the *wabi-sabi* aesthetic found in tea bowls where a master deliberately adds one imperfection to an otherwise perfect creation. Given that the title of my debut memoir is *Accidental Blooms*, I decide to create flower shapes by cutting pink paper and adding them on top of the weaving. It is yet another spontaneous and fortuitous accident, though deviating from Lucy's original instructions.

In that moment, my weaving embodies the essence of *wabi-sabi*—an appreciation for imperfect and incomplete beauty.

Interestingly, each participant interprets Lucy's instructions in their own unique way. Some choose to cut the frame paper in random directions rather than following a single direction, while others have brought recycled paper from home and use them to make a statement. Some, after completing the weaving, add words and drawings directly onto the strips using a pencil. One individual even crinkles paper for both the frame and the threads, resulting in textures that appear almost three-dimensional. In truth, no one adheres precisely to the original instructions of using scissors, curving the frame in one direction, and using pre-cut straight strips. This spirit of experimentation leads to a diverse range of intuitive creations.

I leave the gathering deeply grateful for Lucy and for everyone involved, having witnessed firsthand the powerful role that strong relationships play in nurturing and inspiring creativity. My completed weaving, aptly titled *Coming to Be,* brings profound satisfaction. It symbolizes both my present self, grounded in this moment, and a tantalizing glimpse of what is yet to come. The arts create space for deep listening *and* build relationships, making us fruitful and creative.

At the end of the summer, it is time to disband the filmmaking team, as their employment terms are coming to an end. We have spent the last twelve weeks working closely together, dedicating seven hours every day to our project. It is an emotional moment for all of us. Throughout our process, we often used the phrase "Does that make my eyes shine?" while meticulously editing the film footage and digging deeper into our theme. On our final day, Harry speaks with sincerity, "Keiko, it's been a pleasure working with you. One thing I consistently noticed throughout this project is the sparkle in your eyes. It is truly impressive and memorable. Thank you!"

I am left utterly speechless.

As a naturally caring person, SiMing often has asked me during work, "Keiko, did you eat lunch? Can I get something from your fridge?" I have always felt cared for by the people I worked with, and that is one of the highlights of my project.

I ponder the question: "Did we co-create something novel and exhilarating?" My heart tells me yes.

WHEN HAVE YOU FELT THAT YOU MATTERED?

As I reflect, memories of various conflicts surface—from personal experiences like divorce and break-ups, to witnessing heated local politics unfold in community centres with people shouting and storming out mid-meeting. Since 2020, I've also lost several friends due to disagreements over the legitimacy of Covid vaccines and over discussions about the US presidential election. It seems I'm not alone in navigating these challenging situations. Why can't we find a better way?

In the early days of establishing my artists-in-residence salon at home, I encountered my first challenging situation with an artist, whom I'll refer to as X. X and I had become close friends through family connections. X, a

SALON EVENING
watercolour, 12 × 9

My empty-nest house is all lit up with lights for the evening of the salon and looks as if a giant dragon has awakened from slumber. Moving shadows, lively chatter, the clinking of plates, bursts of laughter, music and clapping—all these sounds and movements breathe life back into the quiet house, creating a magical atmosphere.

full-time artist, enjoyed significant success with almost all his paintings selling out. As the date of his visit to showcase his artworks in my living room drew near, we discussed arrangements to transform the space into a gallery setting.

Upon inspecting the room that was hung with numerous artworks by my now ex–mother-in-law, we counted around eleven or twelve available nails. We decided that we would display the same number of his works on the salon date. However, a few days before the event, X and I met at a cafe for a catch-up. While sipping coffee, X proposed, "Can I come over tomorrow to put new nails on the wall?"

Surprised, I responded, "What? I thought we agreed to use the existing twelve nails on the wall. Remember, we counted them together?" I felt a bit uneasy reminding him of our prior conversation.

X explained, "Keiko, the artwork needs to be at eye level. Depending on the size, we have to adjust the nail heights."

Realizing I had misunderstood his intentions, I apologized, "Oh, I'm sorry. I didn't grasp your intention. I don't think my husband will allow that as we just finished putting his mother's artwork on the wall. Additionally, we're not an art gallery, so I'd appreciate it if you could work within these constraints."

I observed X's expression change; something had gone wrong. He declared, "No way. If I can't install new nails, I'll have to cancel my salon, then!"

In the heat of the moment, I replied, "Okay, then, we should cancel."

An awkward silence lingered, and then X responded, "Please ask your husband when you get home."

I replied, "Okay, but I don't think he will say yes."

That evening, as my now ex-husband Dan was busy boiling pasta in the kitchen, I approached him and said in a troubled tone, "Dan, X's salon is coming up soon, but he asked if we could install new nails for his presentation."

To my surprise, Dan calmly responded, "Well, as long as X puts the wall back exactly the way it is, I'm fine with it."

I was stunned. Was his approval based on X being a family friend? Or was it because Dan, being the son of an artist, was sensitive to an artist's perspective? Knowing him well, it was probably the latter. And that's how X's salon was salvaged. Following the event, X brought stucco and paint to conceal the holes left by those nails. Ironically, even after a decade has passed, I still notice the remnants of that cover-up on my nearly perfect wall, serving as a lasting reminder of the lessons learned. Most conflicts arise because human dignity is overlooked.

For X, his creation is an extension of his spirit. It is crucial to observe and react, understanding that his work holds significance. After reflecting on my words, I realize that the way I responded: "We're not an art gallery," was far from empathetic and respectful. I recognize how I fell short in acknowledging the dignity of others. What if I could express how he and his art mattered? Could this realization have led to a different and better outcome?

After that incident, I became more mindful of the co-creation process, recognizing the potential pitfalls in collaboration. Nonetheless, I often still find myself reflecting on these considerations after the fact rather than in the moment.

Recently, I posed a question to myself: "When have I felt that I truly mattered?" The answer flooded me with gratitude for everything unfolding in my life. The weaving installation process was made so much easier by my friend and collaborator CZarina. She was constantly mindful of my wheelchair, checking in with me regularly: "Keiko, can you reach this easily? Are you doing okay?" Her thoughtfulness made me feel truly cared for and nurtured, and it gave me a profound understanding of what genuine inclusion feels like. I also deeply cherished the moment when Debra Sparrow, my Musqueam weaver friend, graciously acknowledged our friendship, a bond that had blossomed into a collaborative project. Her opening speech at the *Space(s)* exhibition at UBC, in which she highlighted this joint endeavour, was particularly meaningful to me.

Kindness often comes from unexpected places. Andrew, a librarian in Accessible Services, always asks about my day with genuine concern during his regular check-in calls and drop-offs, lifting my spirits. And since the pandemic began, I have received anonymous postcards, often accompanied by drawings, from the volunteers for the Vancouver Public Library Accessible Services. These have been a source of joy and delight and are just the tip of the iceberg. Reflecting, I wonder: When is the last time I made a gesture to others to show that they truly mattered?

OUR DEEPER SENSES

After my book launch, I receive an email from Dr. Paul Steinbok, Professor Emeritus of the Department of Surgery at UBC and a retired pediatric neurosurgeon. We had connected through a community program during the

DILIGENT NATURE
watercolour, 8 × 11

Raising Maya was surprisingly easy. She was incredibly curious, self-disciplined, and diligent, excelling not only academically but also in everyday tasks like grocery shopping. I rarely had to motivate or nudge her. She often anticipated my requests. In retrospect, she was almost too good to be true.

Covid era. His email expresses how impressed he had been by my presentation at my book launch and asks if he could present his work at my salon. I am in awe. Had he read the letter from my daughter included in my first book? The letter ended with her hope that the salon would endure and foster new artists over the years. I express my gratitude to Paul for his thoughtful approach and eagerly set up his salon.

The unexpected connections continue. Numerous friends and acquaintances graciously share their feedback on my book, motivating me to write further, reminding me once again of the inherent self-organizing power of community. Dr. Lorraine Weir, an Emeritus Professor of Indigenous Studies in the Department of English Language & Literatures at UBC, emails me, under the subject line *Volunteering Introduction*, expressing an interest in supporting initiatives of my non-profit organization, the Vancouver Arts Colloquium Society. And this, coupled with her evident intellect and curiosity, leaves a strong impression on me. We arrange to meet for tea soon after. Meanwhile, Tom Sandborn, a respected journalist and writer who reviewed my book, introduces me to a friend, adding, "You both believe in creativity and community, and work to realize those beliefs for yourself and for others."

The connections are snowballing. The moderator of an upcoming literacy festival, after reading my book, reaches out. Though it is an unusual step for her, she asks to connect as friends. We have a meal together and sing a few songs at the end of the evening.

After my book launch, I observe distinct patterns emerging, reminiscent of the way new individuals entered my life when I began living in a wheelchair. This evokes the wisdom of a Japanese saying, そで振り合うも多生の縁 (*Sode furi au mo tashō no en*), which translates to "even the brush of sleeves results from fate in a past life" and emphasizes the significance of every chance encounter. Seeing everyone connect makes me realize how important it is to be open to new people. This leaves a profound impact on me and prompts a fundamental question: What truly shapes the meaning of our lives, especially concerning our impact on the well-being of others? Is it intuition, willpower, or certain tangible sensations?

On the day of Paul's salon, despite a record-breaking snowfall in Vancouver, eighteen people show up to hear about what a neurosurgeon does after retirement. My girlfriend Yvonne arrives a bit early to shovel the snow on the walkway for our guests. Soon, guests start arriving with lively smiles on their pink cheeks, as if they had just come from skiing. They pull off their snow boots and set down their potluck dishes.

Paul's presentation is about his "awe walks," which began during the Covid era. He walks every day in his neighbourhood with the intention of experiencing awe and photographing things that cause him to say, "Wow!" His photography is not only stunningly beautiful but also evident of how he approaches ever-evolving nature with his keen eyes and curious mind, as if he himself becomes one with the sights all around him. I am struck by his systematic investigation of one theme at a time: tree stumps, leaves, bark, windows, rain puddles, drainage ditches. It makes me reflect on how this same methodical approach must inform his work as a neurosurgeon, his dedication to understanding the complexities of the human body.

Ultimately, though, the most profound feelings arise from a deep connection to something living, something that transcends its outward form and speaks to the essence of our lives.

A while ago, my friend David gave me an amaryllis bulb. I plant it in a pot and position it near the kitchen window. With minimal care, the bulb blossoms into four sizable flowers atop a robust stem with luxuriant leaves. I marvel at how a single bulb can hold such energy and vitality.

The once-vibrant flowers soon lose their freshness, turning darker and diminishing in size with each passing day. Typically, I discard plants at this stage, but I find myself unable to do so in this case. Even though its prime beauty has long faded, the amaryllis continues to stand tall, proudly showing its lush green stalks.

Whether I am brewing my morning coffee or washing dishes in the evening, I take a moment to observe the plant, its transformation reminding me of the phases of my own life. Perhaps it is silently imparting lessons on aging and kindness. I feel compelled to witness the amaryllis's existence for as long as its life force lingers. What makes me choose to keep this plant? Is it a curiosity about the culmination of life? Or could it be an innate sense of self-compassion, a gentle acknowledgement of my own impermanence? Or perhaps, simply, the undeniable beauty of the wilted flowers themselves?

For reasons I can't quite pinpoint, I find beauty in the wilting flowers, reminiscent of what Paul might capture through his lens. This newfound appreciation coincides with a subtle shift in my perception of aging bodies and imperfection. Gratitude wells within me. The unique experience of living in a wheelchair has become an integral part of my identity, an identity I now embrace.

Meeting others who are also different allows me to see a shared beauty worth cherishing. That's how I want to live—appreciating everyone's unique beauty. Each connection deepens this understanding.

CCS GOES TO UBC

On Saturday, February 17, 2024, the highly anticipated debut of the CCS (Continuing Continuing Studies) group is at hand. We arrive at the intergenerational dialogue event, Exploring the Future of Human Flourishing, co-developed by UBC's Centre for Community Engaged Learning (CCEL). I invite my fellow CCS members—Lucy, Ela, Eunice, and Alison—to join me as co-creators.

Just one year prior, we were all strangers who happened to meet in a lifelong learning course I taught at SFU. Now, as fellow mid-lifers, we share a bond that transcends individuality. Though our backgrounds are diverse in age, ethnicity, upbringing, marital status, family dynamics, occupations, and personalities, we have formed connections that defy explanation. Who could have foreseen that we would develop into friends, collaborating as a unified team to amplify our voices to the world and engaging in co-learning with younger collaborators to foster collective thriving? We all become staunch advocates for the power of co-creation, recognizing its significance not only as a process but also as a destination. We understand the urgency and importance of forging intergenerational connections, and the others credit me as the catalyst.

I arrive an hour early at the university library. Soon I have settled at a long study desk that is adorned with beautiful lamps, close to our reserved event hall. Around me I notice a few students quietly studying on that long Family Day weekend. Suddenly, I miss Maya. I imagine her sitting somewhere nearby. She used to come to this library to study for her high school graduation exams. I open the book I have brought with me and, instead of practicing my opening presentation as I usually would, I start reading. Today, I feel different—calmer and more confident—not because I have prepared well, but because I believe wholly in the topic of intergenerational co-learning. All I need to do is make sure to not speak flatly, but to let my voice out with emotions.

Before long, Eunice and Lucy arrive. "So exciting!" exclaims Eunice with a big smile. She is wearing a light-yellow cardigan over her black dress.

"I've never seen you wearing anything other than black and white!" I remark.

"I know, I feel like the colour somehow matches my mood today!" she replies in a girlish tone. Lucy appears a bit nervous about her leading role in the paper weaving activity planned after lunch. As a retired after-school teacher, Lucy is the expert in paper weaving and the best person to lead the activity.

The event hall, set with ten rectangular tables, each surrounded by four chairs, quickly fills up with a mix of university students and community members. I am deeply grateful to see so many familiar faces of friends and acquaintances who've supported my events over the years. Among them, I spot my friend, Ben, a retired sociologist. He approaches me and reaches into his backpack. "I found Japanese ramen from your hometown at a grocery," he says with a mischievous smile. Clearly, our community is already in action, improvising and connecting.

I begin my opening speech, "VACS is dedicated to using art to promote self-discovery. When I refer to self-discovery, it's not merely an internal, personal process. It's not solely a cognitive process either. Instead, it's a lived experience, a bodily engagement; it can only be partially articulated, it happens between people, it is 'multimodal,' and it invigorates and transforms people. Our aim is to foster a community that resonates with connection—an authentically and deeply human state..."

I speak calmly yet passionately. I notice a student listening intently, leaning forward, nodding. My eyes keep returning to her, and I feel validated by her engagement.

The morning session flies by. I skip a few slides to allow more time for people to share their thoughts. Those who speak are so passionate and articulate that everyone in the room is captivated. Heads turn, eager to witness the speaker's facial expressions and body language. When is the last time I heard something so deeply heartfelt? I wish I could speak like that spontaneously. Words possess a certain power. Then, I catch myself feeling nervous about the upcoming afternoon art-making session.

The collaborative paper weaving activity aims to visualize our thoughts through abstract art, making the invisible visible. This time, we're adding a collaborative twist: each table will generate a keyword, begin a weaving, and then exchange weavings with other participants at the table to create a seamless, symbolic connection. The success of this abstract art-making hinges on participant engagement. The university has provided a delicious lunch complete with dessert, and I am concerned that people might feel sleepy after eating. As an organizer, I always find it difficult to predict the outcome of such activities. However, I remain optimistic based on past positive experiences.

Lucy speaks with grace and conviction as she gives her instructions. She says, "Trust me, our connections are real, even if invisible." Her humility amplifies her message. Seeing her, I reflect on her dedication to children, a thirty-year commitment to after-school programs. At the age of seventy, she is still full of passion. I hope to feel her vigour and curiosity in my own later years.

Before I know it, all participants are immersed in cutting paper and weaving. The scenes surpass my expectations. Both young and old demonstrate remarkable fluidity in connecting, despite never having met before. I observe plenty of laughter and eye contact among them, as well as the creation of unique and intricate weavings—some even three-dimensional or layered with words and drawings. To conclude the workshop, the final segment is a group presentation, a show-and-tell.

During her group presentation, Claudia, a former student from my course and a dance educator, shares that for her, doing things together is calming, soothing, and grounding. She aptly notes that her engagement is multimodal—a process integrating multiple sensory modalities, such as images, text, spoken language, gestures, and facial expressions.

I am particularly delighted when Claudia uses that term, "multi-modal," a concept I introduced in my opening speech. It is a moment of learning, a sign that the idea has resonated, been internalized, and is now being re-expressed in a new context. Neurons were firing and forming synapses, creating new pathways of understanding. A student on Claudia's team shares her initial struggle with weaving, finding it "primitive." But then she admits it transforms into a calming, childlike experience, reconnecting her with her inner child. She explains that weaving symbolizes intergenerational support, like parents celebrating their children's art, regardless of imperfections. The focus is the experiences, not aesthetics. The ribbon in their weaving represents the thread of life, offering comfort and reassurance in navigating life's challenges.

As I watch this young student, I feel goosebumps. We have never met before, but we have managed to collaborate in such a short time and to create something significant. Through our paper weaving, we are not only connecting with each other but also making our thoughts tangible in a way that words alone cannot express.

A woman in her thirties echoes the student's sentiment, admitting she'd never tried art, let alone weaving. Yet the collaborative design lets her teammates contribute. Surprisingly, she weaves with ease and finds the intergenerational sharing gratifying, even though she is unsure of the final product. She is impressed with how insightful the younger people are. The "waves" in the art are like our own stories and are also what we share, like breathing. She says the best part is the "panic and laughter," and this, to me, highlights the joy of collaboration.

This shows the power of co-creation, and how it helps us grow beyond our limits. Communal learning is also about interpretation. I realize art-based learning reflects our lives and helps us communicate, changing how we see ourselves and our relationships.

During the show-and-tell, I glance at Lucy, who is now standing at the far back of the room. I hope she can feel this wonderful positivity that she helped create rippling through the crowd. After the event, Ela, Alison, Eunice, Lucy, and I gather in a circle and hug each other tightly. A UBC student volunteer, Stephanie, who has been assisting as a co-facilitator with me, tells us, smiling: "Out of all my three years working at CCEL, I have to say that this is my favourite event!" The day leaves such a strong impression on me that I need time to process—to consider how to further develop it. What's next?

WHY I DO WHAT I DO

For the past few years, winter has been a time of reflection and intensive planning as I prepare to teach my annual spring term course at Simon Fraser University's Continuing Studies program. My course, Social Artistry Through Co-Creation, was born out of my passion for using art as a tool for personal and collective transformation. Adopting an inquiry-based, heuristic approach, the course aims to enable lifelong learners to shape their own inquiries and develop seed projects. The purpose is not to create art nor to educate new artists. A more evocative title like "Art-based World-Making" might have been more fitting.

Over the four terms, nearly fifty students from four distinct cohorts successfully completed the program. The students came from diverse professional backgrounds and brought a range of work experiences. Among them were recent retirees exploring new career paths, self-employed artists, and individuals seeking to rediscover old interests or pursue fresh ones. For many of them, enrolling in the course marked a pivotal moment, aligning with significant life transitions such as leaving corporate roles or charting new life directions.

While my first two offerings were more experimental than a fully developed course, the student evaluations were surprisingly positive and kind. As a complete novice to formal teaching, I had no standards for comparison. Reflecting after each term, I wondered if my well-intended, interdisciplinary, haphazard approach was interfering with my ability to connect deeply with the students and the subject matter.

Apropos, while filming the *Hidden Flowers* documentary in the summer of 2023, I was struck by the inspiring story of one of the CCS group members. He had left a thriving career in finance to pursue his passion for acting in mid-life, a journey that ultimately led him to embrace filmmaking as a full-time profession. He firmly believed that the fusion of human creativity and technology democratized art, opening up avenues for creative expression beyond traditional methods. He chose to work independently, quoting the adage "If you want to go fast, go alone; if you want to go far, go together. I want to go fast." Initially drawn to the title of my course but unsure how his solitary creative process aligned with the concept of "social artistry," he found a key insight in the interlocking Individual Change–Collective Change–System Change model I introduced. This framework illuminated how his individual artistic endeavours could contribute to broader social change, providing him with a renewed sense of purpose. He came to realize that he had previously lacked the vocabulary to articulate the connection between his work and its positive social impact.

I am continuing to revise the course, adding and subtracting material, and gradually giving form to vague and fleeting ideas.

I remember reading an academic paper about how people often reinterpret experiences to fit what they already believe about themselves and the world, particularly when something feels off. Figuring out how to reconcile those differences is a key to finding meaning. It seemed like my student was going through something similar, an opportunity to create new meaning. Perhaps we are destined to solve the problems that speak to us when we encounter them by accident. Or perhaps the reverse is true, that we deliberately seek out the mysteries we are meant to unravel. Like many of my students I embrace ambiguity, a recurrent theme in my work.

Summer 2024 arrived, bringing a powerful example of meaning-making in the life of my former student, Greg. My non-profit's new documentary project, *Productive Disruption*, explored local problem solving and intergenerational connections. I invited Greg to join us. Despite his introversion, he agreed, saying, "Something about you makes me unafraid." His Ukrainian and Polish heritage and middle-class upbringing gave him a keen understanding of social inequalities affecting Vancouver's green spaces and the fight against climate change. I asked Greg: *If you could bring about any change in the world right now, what would it be?* In response, Greg created art using a most unusual canvas—a majestic, 170-year-old beech tree that stood in front of his house. This magnificent tree, "loved by some and loathed by others," as Greg said, was under threat from some of his neighbours, who, eager to improve their view, had even offered to pay for its removal—a familiar battle in Vancouver.

Instead of resorting to argument, Greg chose a more creative path. He began by painting a bright white circle with tree-safe latex paint on the front of the trunk. The circle, suggestive of a three-dimensional cylinder, was intended, he said, to "assist people to look through the trunk, through the branches, through the leaves, through to the other side, to *view* whatever we can imagine." He named it *The View*. To me, it was a "portal" straight out of science fiction—a way to perceive possible futures and grasp the interconnectedness of the universe.

Inspired by Greg's unique approach, I proposed to co-create a community dialogue to explore fundamental questions of identity: who we are, how we got here, and what possibilities lie before us. We then documented the process by inviting community members, including his own neighbours, to engage in "see-think-wonder" conversations through informal street chats and more structured cultural salons. The varied interpretations of Greg's tree art aptly demonstrated the subjective nature of perception. It was particularly gratifying to witness Greg's reaction when one participant exclaimed, "A portal-like opening to see through!" Greg's burst of laughter spoke volumes, revealing his delight at this unexpected recognition of his artistic intent.

Greg's portal served as a catalyst, opening our perspectives and allowing us to safely and critically explore the far-reaching impact of the income gap on urban planning and green spaces, the lingering influence of colonialism, the constantly evolving nature of community, and the profound ways in which these factors affect our collective and individual well-being. Greg eloquently articulated his vision: "I just want to give more of what I have. If I could go through the 'portal,' I want to continue to be more nature." This, I realized, was the very essence of art-based world-making—the creation of a shared vision for a more just and sustainable future. One participant, capturing the spirit of our conversation, echoed this sentiment with a simple yet resonant phrase: "All our relations."

Looking back, I see how crucial relationships are to co-creation—that interplay of beauty, meaning, and emotion. For my future teaching and non-profit work, fostering wonder and nurturing relationships will be key to tackling challenges like climate change and social isolation. Little Richard's words, "I think that a man should be caring," say it all.

THE RHYTHM OF NOW

Even a week after experiencing *Perfect Days*, the film continues to affect me, prompting ongoing conversations with friends who have also seen it. The film seems to have awakened my right brain, enabling me to dwell in the Japanese concept of *ma*—that pregnant pause in time, that emptiness within space. It's the aesthetic concept of the space between that gives form and meaning to the whole. Mr. Hirayama, as portrayed in the film, embodies the essence of *ma* seamlessly navigating through everyday life without halting his movements. *Perfect Days* has given me precisely what I am searching for: a deeper understanding of *ma* and a desire to integrate it into every facet of my life, from my work to my relationships, to find the natural pauses.

On an early spring day, as I return from the post office, I opt to take a detour to the nearby park instead of heading straight home. Though the weather is a bit chilly, with cloudy skies hinting at rain, I feel compelled to explore. Entering the forest trail I frequent during the summer and early fall, I am struck by how different it appears—the once lush trees and bushes are now bare, stripped of their leaves, casting the familiar landscape in a new light. In the soft, diffused sunlight, unobstructed by the foliage, I see the dirt trail winding ahead, disappearing around the bend. I catch a familiar scent in the air; it is reminiscent of dampness and decomposition, yet oddly comforting.

As I proceed in my motorized wheelchair, I find the park eerily quiet, devoid of people. The soft hum of the tires on the now-dried ground is the only break in the silence. Pausing to survey the marshes, I notice the remnants of the recent storm—old trees uprooted and scattered across the bog in diagonal patterns. My attention is drawn to the dark water, which seems to come alive with shimmering light, casting abstract reflections of the surrounding tree branches. In the distance, beyond the horizon, a lush green field unfolds, while above, blue sky peeks through the clouds. Captivated, I grab my phone and capture the view where the bog mirrors the world above—or perhaps below—in its depths.

Then, the sun breaks through. Suddenly, the once subdued trails and parks burst with vibrancy, as if I'd learned to amplify the world's saturation. I find myself capturing many pictures of the park, seeing it anew. What is meant to be a brief detour turns into an hour-long ramble. Emerging from the park, I am remarkably relaxed, free from specific thoughts or worries.

Returning home, I carry the calm of the forest with me, entering the familiar quiet. Instead of loneliness, I sense that the house is awaiting my arrival. Is it just my cheeks warmed by the heated air inside? Or is it a genuine anticipation? In the distance, I spot my cat Pumpkin bounding towards me, her tail held upright in joyful enthusiasm. "*Tadaima*, Pumpkin!" I call out, announcing my arrival. Inside, my reflection greets me in the entrance mirror, a silent and familiar cheerleader. Pumpkin urges me to the kitchen for her treat. Chuckling, I remark, "*Kawaii ne!*" (So cute!), engaging in our playful ritual. She's always ready for life, no matter what.

I reheat last night's dinner and eat alone, quietly content. I grab Murakami's latest novel, *The City and Its Uncertain Walls*, and eagerly dive back into it. Just six months ago, in the aftermath of Maya's departure, this solitary evening might have seemed miserable—even if shared with some friends. But now, to my surprise, for the first time, I feel a sense of peace and autonomy. I am the master of my destiny, the conductor of my orchestra. Like Mr. Hirayama, I am already in *ma*—the silence between notes that gives music its rhythm. I just need to stay open to possibilities and embrace the repetition inherent in life's natural rhythms.

The following week, my former film intern, Harry, a twenty-three-year-old Korean Canadian, joins me for coffee. He has just returned from travels in England and Korea. Five months since our last meeting, we enjoy a three-hour conversation spanning work, culture, relationships, and more. With his keen observational skills and eloquent expression, he remarks, "Keiko, your eyes look different, more relaxed, especially when you speak about Maya."

"Well, that's a change!" I respond, cherishing his words as a testament to my evolution over the course of the last five months.

MAKE DO

My desk is becoming increasingly cluttered, a classic case of *tsundoku*—the Japanese practice of acquiring reading materials without reading them. I have always thought this is a modern word, but the term, a combination of *tsumu* (積む, to pile up) and *doku* (読, reading), originated in the Meiji Era (1868–1912). Who knew? The Japanese have a knack for coining new words to describe unique cultural concepts. Crucially, *tsundoku* isn't necessarily a negative term; it's more akin to a love of books, rather than hoarding.

My piled-up books look like a miniature Inukshuk, balancing precariously atop each other: *Japanese Myths and*

Tales, *The Art of Fermentation*, Joy Kogawa's *The Lost and Found Department,* and *Collective Wisdom*, a few Japanese paperback classics, *Impressionist Artists* (in Japanese), *Resilience*, *The City and Its Uncertain Walls*, *The Korean Peninsula and Japan's Future* (in Japanese), and *Like Mother, Like Mother.* It seems random, defying any discernible theme, and yet it is a tangible representation of my mind's wanderings and interests over the past year. What sense can I make of this eclectic mix? The only pattern I can discern is the chronological order in which they are stacked.

These books, some barely touched, others well-worn, have been either gifted to me or carefully selected and purchased. Despite their varied origins, they have all been present on my desk throughout the year, serving as both a testament to my habitual *tsundoku* and a support for my personal evolution, consciously or not. While working at my desk, I must have glanced countless times at their spines—their designs, letter styles, and titles. Their seeming randomness is an invitation to serendipitous discovery and a potential generator of illuminating juxtapositions, like a lost and found.

Just then, Levi-Strauss's concept of the *bricoleur* comes to mind. Like the Meiji-era Japanese who coined the term *tsundoku*, we often engage in *bricolage* (tinkering), piecing together existing ideas and materials to create something new. The very act of coining the word *tsundoku* is itself a form of *bricolage*, literally and figuratively. It's a way of collecting and storing potential resources for future inspiration.

I increasingly embrace the role of a *bricoleur* in both my work and personal life. Without a predefined curriculum or a rigid life script, I'm compelled to experiment and create new adventures from my own lived experiences. Inspired by figures like my grandparents or by Haruki Murakami (one of my favourite writers), I look for unique ways to connect with the world around me.

Recently, I experienced a significant loss with the passing of Saskia, a dear friend and founding member of our weaving group. She passed away at the age of seventy-five after a battle with cancer, just two weeks after her last attendance at our group meet-up.

We knew about Saskia's cancer diagnosis for several years, and she had been on palliative care for the past few months. Despite her unimaginable physical and emotional challenges, she never lost her curiosity, kindness, and commitment to our weaving group. The only visible trace of her struggle was the weight she had lost, though even then a certain handsomeness shone through. I've never met anyone quite like her, except perhaps my own mother, who displayed similar resilience in the face of adversity. Saskia was always eager to help novice weavers, to create her unique pieces, and to express her admiration for the work of others.

The last time I saw her was at our regular weaving meet-up. Only she knew it would be her final attendance. Instead of her usual weaving project, she brought a felting needle and a bag of leftover yarn scraps, saying with a big smile, "This is manageable, as long as I don't prick myself!" Her fingers moved steadily as she worked. She also deeply affirmed how much the group meant to her and how much she enjoyed our camaraderie. "I'm reading your book for the second time," she said to me, "and I'm really getting a lot out of it." I believe she was referring to the part where I wrote about my mother's experience with cancer. Saskia thoughtfully brought copies of the group photos we had taken a month or two earlier, giving one to each member of the group.

Two weeks after that, I received the devastating news of her death. Her infectious smile, her cheerful voice, her nimble fingers deftly working her felting, and the warmth of her kind eyes flooded into my mind. Above all, it was her unwavering equanimity in the face of adversity that I recalled. She radiated not just acceptance, but also joy, deep gratitude, resilience, and beauty. She inspired deep reflection on the meaning of our lives.

We leave our imprint in so many ways, through our actions and deeds. To leave a legacy of enduring love and the courage to overcome fear—this, perhaps, is her most profound gift.

Saskia embodied the spirit of the *bricoleur*, not just in her art, but in her life. She had a remarkable ability to adapt, to improvise, to create something beautiful from whatever circumstances presented. This is evident in all her ventures, from the practical—such as the ingenious bicycle door she installed in her garage to save electricity, a move she proudly declared "very Dutch"—to the deeply personal. Her weavings are equally personal, often depicting scenes from her neighbourhood or cherished moments from her past. She often shared her thoughts on my VACS newsletter. In 2020, during the pandemic, she contributed to our visual journaling project, a collaborative artist book titled, *In Search of Our Creative Edge,* writing:

> I came from the Netherlands and have a great need to belong in Canada. For years I have been a potter in a club, and the weaving craft is a huge addition to my creative expression and sharing of common ground with other immigrants. The suggestion of journaling added and deepened the thought of expression and helped me deal with the year 2020, where the shock of living in a pandemic turned our lives upside down.
>
> When I was young, I kept journals from time to time, adding magazine photos, and made scrapbooks of my favourite movie stars. I now see the value of expressing one's feelings in a creative way. It is a form of release for me and an ongoing evaluation of where I am at, and where I hope to go. There is a constant dialogue with what I feel like sharing and what I keep private. I see the great value of sharing with others as I have learned so much from other people. VACS, and especially Keiko, but also other people have shown me the value of all creative endeavours.

"Life is on hold but not over! Remember your friends, embrace the outdoors." These words she added to our collaborative book even as she faced her own mortality. This was not mere rhetoric; it is the very essence of how she lived.

Saskia was a true comrade. Her life exemplified the transformative power of creative pursuits. In her memory, I continue to make do, drawing strength from resourcefulness. On my desk is a photo she generously printed of our weaving group—a small celebration of our shared *tsundoku* that reminds me daily to celebrate her through *bricolage*.

SIX

EMBRACING SEASONS

冬至 (**TŌJI**), **WINTER SOLSTICE**
watercolour, 9 × 12

Winter is a precious season for me, a time for quiet contemplation and for reflecting on the lessons I've learned. It's a period of recalibration as I prepare myself for the new year that lies ahead. There's a saying in Japan that if you eat pumpkin on the winter solstice, you won't catch a cold. Honestly, I just crave it in the cold. Pumpkin soup is definitely a winter staple at my place.

時節感当

Sensing the season,
seizing the timing.

ZEAMI MOTOKIYO

SEASONS CHANGE. Soon a year will have passed since my daughter Maya's departure, a turning point in my life. Have I managed to maintain the heart connection that bound me to my daughter, my family, and my community, despite the inevitable silences and missteps? Just as our ancestors are attuned to the subtle shifts of the twenty-four seasons, I have tried to chronicle my inner seasons through writing. Zeami's concept of *jisetsu kantō*, a profound awareness of the fleeting moment serves as a constant reminder to seize opportunities as they arise and to live each day with intention.

This focus on meaning resonates deeply with something my friend Dr. Robert Woollard, a retired physician and Emeritus

Professor of Family Medicine at UBC, once shared with me. He observed, "Having treated many patients throughout my lifetime, one thing I've learned is the connection between longevity and a person's sense of meaning. No matter how difficult or devastating the circumstances, those who hold onto their sense of meaning tend to fare better. However, the moment we lose our sense of meaning, our body begins to give up on itself. We cannot afford to delay the search for meaning."

These words underscore the importance of connection, purpose, and the intentional living that *jisetsu kantou* encourages. In other words: seize the right moment. As I navigate this new season, I strive to embody both, cherishing the fleeting moments and holding fast to the meaning they create.

MY FIRST CHRISTMAS POST-MAYA

I've been in emotional turmoil ever since Maya's surprise announcement in early September that she wouldn't be staying with me over the holidays, but that she would instead stay at her boyfriend Micah's. Some parents and grandparents reassure me that their daughters and granddaughters did the same but that they eventually returned when they matured. While I am still tormented by doubt, I know there is nothing I can do other than love her more.

The initial experience of empty nesting can be compared to a sudden emptiness. But it's a much more complex transition than I anticipated. Maya's distance has prompted deep reflection on my role as a mother and the intricacies of our mother–daughter relationship. I long for a simple acknowledgement, even a "Hi, Mom!" as I navigate this new phase. Each time I find myself submerged in self-doubt and disappointment, I attempt to brush these feelings aside, but they inevitably return. Gradually, however, a new perspective is beginning to emerge.

As the first Christmas since her departure draws near, I devise a plan to stay productive. Partly, this involves preparing for an upcoming winter house concert, a joint effort organized by Maya's best friend Jocelyn. However, as the event approaches, I learn that Maya won't be attending due to Micah's coinciding birthday party. Ugh!

Despite my reserved nature, I make an unconventional decision: to perform a Japanese song for the audience, marking my debut public performance. This way I can make the occasion more joyful to offset the disappointment of Maya's absence. Sometimes negative feelings provide good motivation.

I enlist the help of Gerard, Maya's former piano teacher, to provide piano accompaniment. And my Japanese friend, also named Keiko, agrees to play the flute. From the Japanese karaoke database, I select *Zankoku na Tenshi no Te-ze* (*A Cruel Angel's Thesis*), a song known for its vocal challenges: a fast tempo, significant range, complex melody, and a demanding *a cappella* opening.

I spend the weeks preceding the concert honing my singing abilities by diligently studying karaoke tutorials and YouTube voice training videos. My focus is primarily on refining my pitch and mastering the challenging art of breath control. To monitor my progress, I make a habit of recording every practice session, meticulously listening to identify imperfections.

Seeking precious feedback, I share multiple versions with both my family and my muse, Gabriel. My father, surprised by the recording, admits he'd never heard me sing and humorously describes my singing as "interesting," implying it might not match his taste. The rest of my supporters offer generous feedback. I recognize there is still plenty of room for improvement.

Pumpkin, my cat, has grown so used to my singing that she barely twitches her ears when I start, unlike her first startled responses. I attempt to capture her attention by singing louder, but she just dozes off. I interpret it as a signal of our newly established routines.

Through daily repetition, I memorize all the lyrics. I progress to practicing in front of mirrors, aiming to synchronize my facial expressions with the lyrics, even though the audience will not comprehend the Japanese words. Emotions must resonate through both the voice and facial cues. Engrossed in this unfamiliar self-directed training, I gradually notice improvements in both pitch and breath control.

Imagining an audience enjoying the music fuels my determination to improve. I remember Zeami's apropos notion of hidden flowers (the aesthetics of the concealed and unexpected). The audience will not only be surprised by my appearance as a performer but also by my choice of a rhythmic Japanese pop song. I chuckle at the unlikely mix of elements, considering it a surprise gift to the audience. I am both excited and nervous. Is this how Maya felt about her class presentations—worried beforehand, but totally ready a week early?

The much-awaited concert day arrives. Our guests are to be greeted at the door by a volunteer distributing beautifully printed programs. We are thrilled to have received twenty-eight RSVPs, among whom are courageous performers of diverse ages and cultural backgrounds. The musical ensemble includes piano, guitar, flute, and trumpet.

Leading up to the event, Gerard, Keiko-san, and I can only manage a single rehearsal a week prior. Evaluating our performance, I'd gauge it at around 70 percent in terms of artistic delivery. Although I want another rehearsal before the guests arrive, my responsibilities take over;

I have to welcome guests and prepare special surprise birthday cakes for my younger friends, Marvel and Isabel, two UBC students. Before I know it, the room is filled with heightened anticipation.

"Good evening everyone and welcome to our Cozy Winter Concert!" I announce through the microphone. Joycelyn and her friend take the stage. Witnessing the performers pour their hearts into their craft moves me deeply. The audience reciprocates with support and enthusiasm, often sharing lighthearted moments that have us all bursting with laughter.

I have scheduled my performance toward the event's conclusion, just before the final sing-along, and I now nervously await my turn. As I prepare, I speak a few words, testing the microphone. My practice sessions were in an empty room where echoes reverberate; but in this packed room, I sense that the sound will be different. With no time to adjust, we press ahead.

Despite unexpected technical issues that prevent me from hearing my singing voice precisely, our performance earns us resounding applause, even from the anchor choir. As much as I try to cherish every moment to preserve it in my memory, time slips away, and the song concludes faster than I had anticipated. Left in its wake are feelings of immense relief and a yearning for more experiences like this in the future: singing, creating music alongside friends, and sharing it with our guests.

The evening continues to engage the audience, even after two hours. "Open mic! Who's next?" I announce. A young man steps forward. He plays the piano and sings a song close to his heart. Despite a few missed and forgotten notes, his rendition deeply moves the audience. But it is his heartfelt words afterward that truly captivate us. He expresses gratitude for the supportive and welcoming atmosphere, explaining that it had given him the courage to share his song publicly for the first time, despite his lifelong shyness. His sincere expression of vulnerability and appreciation moves everyone present.

A month ago, when I began organizing this concert, I had no clue how it would unfold, especially considering my sorrow over Maya's absence. But, happily, the power of co-creation drives our success. This winter concert serves as a testament to the beauty of a community coming together through art. Next time, count me in.

NEW BEGINNING, NEW YEAR

On New Year's morning, just after waking, I receive a fresh email from my dear friend, Joy Kogawa—the renowned Japanese-Canadian poet and novelist, best known for her Canadian classic, *Obasan*, whose work has significantly affected Canadian literature and raised awareness about the history of Japanese Canadians. Her words touch me: "Dearest Keiko, you show so many of us how to be. Thank you for the light in your beautiful face, in your mothering, in your energy. Blessings for the new year."

Her message glows with humility and tranquil grace. I picture her, sitting alone in her Toronto apartment and

CHERISHED TRADITION
pencil, 12 × 9

Sunday at six o'clock is sacred; it is my weekly FaceTime call with Maya and Micah. We've established a cherished tradition of ending the call with a quick screenshot. Now, I have nearly fifty of these precious selfies—a visual chronicle of our evolving relationship, and a source of immense gratitude for these two young adults in my life.

composing this message of warmth. It feels like a precious gift, a quiet affirmation from a woman who has profoundly influenced my own understanding of what it means to be human, a woman who has taught so many of us how to simply "be and be courageous." Her New Year's greeting is more than just a kind gesture; it is a gentle lesson in kindness, a reminder of the power of seeing the good in others, and a testament to the enduring strength of a life lived with purpose and compassion. In the quiet of my home, I, too, embrace solitude, savouring the peace of mind I've discovered since reuniting with Maya over this winter break.

Though I was initially saddened by Maya's decision to spend the first winter break at her boyfriend's home instead of "our" home, the moment I saw her, my heart opened and softened, as if nothing had changed. Sitting at the breakfast table on Christmas, sipping coffee, we chatted about her new university life, sharing girl-talk. She was still the same Maya, with her endearing cheeks and mischievous smiles. Her signature superpower—the curious mind—was on full display. She unwrapped her Christmas gift, *Humanly Possible*, listed as one of Barack Obama's favourite books of 2023, and carefully read the blurb on the book jacket. "This sounds fascinating! I can't wait to dive into it," she exclaimed. Her eyes, gleaming with excitement, fixed on mine.

In that instant, all my anxieties melted away. I saw the incredible person she has become, and my faith in our bond was renewed. "Well, enjoy the read. Keep that curiosity alive. Then, you're set for life!" I said, smiling.

Our brief, happy reunion on Christmas stretches through New Year's Day, a fleeting week that somehow holds an eternity of meaning. How does such a simple moment of eye contact wield such transformative power? What sparks this deep connection? I want to understand the alchemy of this moment, the shift in my heart.

Then a phrase I heard countless times from my grandmother echoes in my memory: "A child does a lifetime's worth of filial piety by the age of three." It's a saying that always seems to carry a deeper meaning than its literal translation. It's not about excusing a child's later "misbehaviour," but recognizing the profound and unconditional love a young child offers, a love that is its own reward. It's a reminder, perhaps, that the purest form of giving is simply *being*, a lesson easily forgotten amid the pressures of raising a child in a complex world. Even though I knew this, somewhere along the way, I may have forgotten the deep wisdom passed down through generations of mothers and grandmothers. I may have fallen prey to the subtle anxieties of parenthood, the unspoken expectations, the fear of somehow failing to nurture her potential. This moment, this simple connection, reminds me of that fundamental truth: that love, in its purest form, is enough. It's a gentle nudge back to the wisdom of generations, a reminder to cherish the present and trust in the unfolding of her unique journey. And in that trust, I find my own peace.

When our gazes lock, a feeling of revelation floods over me, magical and inexplicable. It may be a cliché to say that "the eyes are the windows to the soul," but in her gaze, I can see all the way through to her clear, intelligent, and kind nature. She glows with graceful tranquility, embodying the wisdom of Joy Kogawa's New Year's message. I sense a new phase in our relationship, a new phase of my life and my unwavering love for her.

I reflect on the insights I gained from my interactions with both Maya and Micah this winter. Despite the differences in the dynamics of these two significant relationships, a fundamental value resonates strongly: trust, and the simple joy of placing that trust. What more could I ask for on New Year's Day? Blessings for the new year, as Joy Kogawa would say.

The next day, Maya and Micah join me for dinner. I organize an experiment for them. I aim to evoke the surprising joy of co-creation in these young lovebirds. My maternal instinct spurs me to give them a space to relax and to engage something new. After a lively meal, we migrate to a room I've prepared with a large blank canvas, acrylic paints, and brushes. We brainstorm a theme for the new year. Micah, being a native Chinese, shares a proverb that translates to: "Dispel the clouds and see the sun."

We all appreciate his insight, envisioning the sun as a symbol of truth and clarity for the year ahead. Their idea is to draw the sun at the centre and freely explore with colours. I play Maya's favourite background music—Studio Ghibli's piano tunes—and quietly observe the magic unfolding. I savour each moment as, for the first time, these two bright university students collaborate in a visual medium, sharing their thoughts and emotions through art.

I watch them submerge in the moment, and I happily note the sparkle in Maya's eyes. She is still my child, of course, but she has also blossomed into a beautiful woman. After some painterly progress, I suggest they switch positions, each to continue the other's painting: "Try harmonizing your collaborative work despite your distinct styles!" This poses the question I have often pondered in my own work: How can I authentically express myself while embracing the authenticity of others?

I observe their brushstrokes more attentively. Maya's strokes morph to emulate his style as she continues in the empty spaces of his painting. Meanwhile, by looking from different angles, Micah inflects the given shapes, then truncates his strokes to dots, blending multiple colours in a new technique, superimposing them over Maya's compositions. Their approaches are distinctly different. "Oh no! Please don't change my clouds!" Maya exclaims, worried he might paint over them entirely. He reassures her he won't. His dotted strokes render a three-dimensional effect with vibrant colours, maintaining the exact shape of Maya's clouds. Maya is surprised. "Wow! I like it!"

I experience a revelation as I witness their unexpected and beautiful co-creation: they value not just the outcome but the process. As they swap positions to continue each other's paintings, I observe how their attentiveness heightens. This reaffirms my belief that effective community co-creation demands careful observation and an openness to other perspectives, factors that aren't as apparent when people work individually.

After completing their artwork, they sign their names, write the Chinese proverb that provided the work, then date it. We hang the work in my entrance hall. The radiant yellow sun now graces my view, serving as a reminder of precious memories and New Year's resolutions.

EPIGENETIC

I learn that Maya and Micah have joined the Hart House Singers, a non-auditioned choir at the University of Toronto known for singing a culturally and historically diverse repertoire. Apparently, Maya initiated this, persuading Micah to join her. This comes as a delightful surprise, especially considering Maya's previous reservations about performing in public, reservations that had only intensified as she grew older. Despite their busy extracurricular lives—writing for the student newspaper, *Trinity Times*, and participating in the Trinity College Multicultural Society—they are thoroughly enjoying this new musical outlet.

Maya's involvement in the choir is particularly intriguing, given her musical background. She has been learning piano since the age of five and has showcased her talent in numerous house concerts, where she played piano and guitar (self-taught) and sang pop songs. Given her perfect pitch and beautiful voice (admittedly I am biased), Maya's involvement in the choir seems to be an exciting development in her artistic journey.

The day of the Hart House Spring Season Concert has finally arrived. The university has made provisions for those unable to attend in person by sending a Zoom link for live-streaming the performance. I set up my laptop. I can barely contain my excitement as I bring my lunch plate and Pumpkin's serving bowl over and then text Maya: "Pumpkin and I got the first-row seats!" With a full orchestra, the hour-and-a-half program features Mozart's *Requiem* and other classical music. Experiencing a concert through Zoom truly embodies the ethos of the post-pandemic era. Pumpkin is already enjoying her snack before the opening notes. Good for her!

The Zoom screen changes from the cover page to the live camera view of the concert hall. I am struck by its resemblance to the grandeur of Hogwarts in the Harry Potter films. The hall is tall and expansive with arched stained-glass windows serving as a backdrop, bathing the space in warm, natural light. Towering stone pillars stretch towards a ceiling of intricate woodwork, and crystal chandeliers shimmer, casting a brilliant glow. Along the walls, college crests line the space, evoking the time-honoured tradition and academic prestige of East Coast universities. Even through the virtual medium, I feel transported, as if seated among the audience. Keen to capture every nuance, I turn the volume to its highest setting.

The orchestra members begin to tune their instruments, creating a cacophony of sound that gradually melds into a harmonious melody. The tuning process concludes and now the singers, clad in black formal attire, solemnly enter the room. Amidst the ensemble, I spot Maya, her diminutive stature making her stand out. I cheer loudly through my laptop, "Maya!!" causing Pumpkin to startle and leap off the table. With great anticipation, we all await the first notes.

Throughout the entire performance, the tip of my nose tingles. I imagine a sense of unity and purpose among the musicians contributing to the creation of perfect harmony in that majestic room. They create such exquisite sounds—a gift for others to enjoy. Transcendence! Keeping my eyes fixed on Maya's tiny face on the computer screen, I imagine her immersed in the ecstatic performance, appearing to reach a personal apotheosis as she sings, and silently acknowledging her parents watching from a distance. Gratitude for Maya fills my thoughts, warm tears stream down my cheeks.

My thoughts then turn to my own parents. Moving from Japan to New York meant losing frequent connection. No Wi-Fi, no iPhones, no Zoom. Expensive landline calls and snail mail were our only links, with an annual trip home our sole in-person exchange. They missed so much of my twenties and thirties. I imagine what might have been if we'd had Zoom or iPhones three decades earlier. Perhaps much sorrow could have been avoided.

My childhood was rich with artistic experiences, thanks to the influence of my grandparents and mother, whose own lives were deeply immersed in art. Watching my grandfather read and write in the living room, tend to his garden, and paint in his atelier became part of my daily life. My grandmother's skills in mending, flower arranging, cooking, and keeping her house impeccably clean and organized inspired me. My mother was always singing and dancing—modern ballet and other styles. They engaged in a wide range of artistic pursuits, refusing to be limited to a single medium, much like samurai in the feudal period.

I cherish every detail of my upbringing in my grandparents' home, vividly recalling memories that shape who I am today. They epitomized love, compassion, and kindness, leaving a lasting impact on all who knew them. My mother often said, "You embody kindness because you were raised by your grandparents," a testament to their profound impact.

Writing my memoir, *Accidental Blooms*, and revisiting these memories has been a rejuvenating and nourishing experience, fostering within me a deeper compassion for myself and others. This transformation was organic, and I believe that appreciation is the key—a simple virtue.

This lasting impact, this inheritance, recalls the concept of epigenetics. Epigenetics is the idea that our experiences and exposures can actually change how our genes work even without changing the DNA itself, like worker bees and the queen bee—genetically identical, but shaped by their environment and by something as simple as diet. Perhaps, like royal jelly, the love and kindness I received from my grandparents acted as an epigenetic influence, shaping not just my outlook, but perhaps something deeper.

Like me, Maya has benefited from a lifelong engagement with art and community. Inspired by my own upbringing, I tried to create an environment for her that was rich in artistic expression. She spent many evenings in a vibrant salon culture where dialogue about various art forms was actively encouraged. I like to think that this environment, shaped by numerous individuals who played a significant role in her development, has helped her excel across the sciences, arts, and humanities. Her studies at the University of Toronto are now enriched by her new involvement in the Hart House Singers.

From my laptop I hear the rising harmonic progression of the *Dies irae* (*Day of Wrath*), a profoundly ominous and dramatic movement. The music surges forth with thunderous drumbeats and soaring vocal lines, evoking a sense of urgency, alarm, and an almost ecstatic intensity. The music elicits a visceral response. I sit spellbound, motionless, and unblinking, yet it feels as if my heart beats in perfect sync with the music's rhythm. Imagine being in the same room as the musicians!

The concert concludes with a grand fanfare, and I applaud vigorously, hoping my enthusiasm reaches Maya's heart. Reflecting on the experience, I ponder our future. I don't want to wait thirty years for a teleporter so we can make more memories together.

Given our distance, how can we enhance each other's vitality? As the echoes of the performance linger, I contemplate the effect we have on each other, whether intentional or not. The word "epigenesis" is stuck in my head. I keep hearing the phrase: "Creation on top of creation, on top of creation, on top of creation." This is a phrase I heard from Dr. Pille Bunnell, a reputable cybernetist with whom Maya and I have become close family friends. During our interview on epigenesis in 2018, she offered insights into the way a lineage of moments influences our development, often in ways we can't fully anticipate. She emphasized the importance of integrity, stating that it involves being clear about holding onto whatever is relevant as we continue along our continuous path, with each moment changing who we are.

I consider: how can we intentionally harness epigenesis or epigenetic plasticity rather than leaving it to chance? By nurturing our integrity and engaging with art, can we deliberately shape our development? I see it in my own life, I see it in Maya. I see it in our shared history.

MY ORDINARY DAY

A week prior, at the Accessible Arts and Culture Forum hosted by the Disability Foundation (where I was attending as a board member and panelist), I encountered Kamille, an IT specialist hailing from Iran. Following the forum, Kamille reached out via email, expressing his interest in meeting for coffee and conversation. His email was delightful.

We settle in for our coffee meeting. Kamille sips his matcha latte before expressing his thoughts. "When I begin to learn about you and your life's work," he says, "I realize that is exactly what I aspire to be and do." I notice that he has brought along a copy of my memoir. The copy has Post-it notes between its pages. Even more surprising, the book is laminated!

Though taken aback by his remark, I feel compelled to ask. "Really? What makes you say that?" I inquire, my curiosity piqued by the stark contrasts between us—culture, religion, areas of expertise, gender, and disability status, to name just a few. I continue, "You've been in the IT industry for quite some time; you must excel at what

A BLOOM BY OUR SIDE
watercolour, 12 × 9

Throughout the seasons, my flower vases remain ever ready to welcome the blooms of each new season. I often reflect on how much more vibrant our lives are because of the beauty and joy that flowers bring to our homes and our hearts.

you do. Could you share a bit about your current role and how you got started in this field?"

With a smile, he responds, "Well, how far back do you want me to go?" He then proceeds to recount his journey.

Growing up in Iran, he frequently visited his aunt's home where she, a literature professor at the university, surrounded herself with books. Her desk was strewn with open volumes and papers, and, as she had low vision, she relied on a magnifying glass to navigate through them. Eleven-year-old Kamille often assisted her in finding what she needed. One day, he had an idea: to develop a software solution that would simplify her search process. And so, at that young age, he designed both the hardware and software to address this issue. This early innovation sparked his interest in technology.

He pursued his passion by studying electrical engineering and computer hardware at university. Following graduation, he began his career as an adaptive technology specialist. Today, he holds a senior management position in digital accessibility development at a major Canadian bank.

Listening to his story, it becomes clear that his deep commitment to assisting individuals with disabilities was the driving force behind his participation in the forum. He elaborates, "I've been passionate about my work since that time. Providing solutions for the blind and those with low vision has always been my calling and foundation." It is evident that he has translated his vision into tangible and impactful action.

Now he reaches into his backpack and remarks, "I have something for you. I hope you'll like it." At that he sets two gifts onto the table. One is square. One is cylindrical. Both are elegantly wrapped with Japanese, flower-patterned *washi* paper.

"Wow! I'm not sure what to say! May I?" I respond bashfully and eagerly open the cylindrical gift first.

The *washi* paper feels authentic and possesses a distinct weight and texture that evokes a familiar and nostalgic tactile sensation. "Where did you find these beautiful papers?" I inquire as I unwrap the gift. He responds with a smile, "I bought them at a Japanese store as they perfectly complement the themes of *Accidental Blooms*!" My eyes widen in wordless astonishment.

Inside the *washi* paper, I discover a delicate bouquet of dried flowers. "I purchased them at the UBC farms. They're locally sourced," he explains. His thoughtfulness is impressive, especially considering he has transported them in his backpack while bicycling, ensuring they remained unharmed. I express my gratitude for his kindness, time, and effort.

As I reach for the second gift, I find a book by Brené Brown, titled *Atlas of the Heart*. She is an author whom I deeply admire. Opening the accompanying card, I behold an oversized print of Hokusai's *Great Wave.* He apparently obtained it from the Seattle Art Museum during its recent Hokusai exhibition. In his card, he writes:

> To Dear Keiko,
>
> You are a true force of nature. You not only sailed your boat through breaking waves of life and brought it back to tranquil shores, but since then you've been going back to the ocean helping others sail safely to the shores of love and peace. You have my immense respect.

I am captivated by the exquisite beauty of the card and moved by his heartfelt words, words that show his artistic sensibility through metaphor. Throughout our conversation, he expresses admiration for my courage and bravery. I wonder what he meant. Was it the vulnerability of writing a memoir, laying my life bare on the page? Or was it my commitment to the non-profit world, the effort to build something from the ground up? Or perhaps . . . was it the quiet strength of living, of embracing life's fullness, even from a wheelchair?

His written words, "going back to the ocean helping others sail safely," not only reflect his perception of me but also echo the journey of his own life. Unpacking the compliments bestowed upon me is a humbling experience. It becomes clear that they are not solely about me; rather, they offer a glimpse into the soul of the person offering the compliment. Additionally, it becomes evident that sharing our authentic voices has the power to bring people from diverse backgrounds together and foster a sense of belonging.

A key insight from our conversation is the powerful sense of joy and encouragement I feel simply from the genuine appreciation of company. It highlights the profound impact of simply enjoying another person's presence, without any ulterior motive. I realize this is a crucial point I could have shared during the Accessible Arts and Culture Forum. When addressing equity and inclusion, we must move beyond prescribed standards to embrace the inherent joy of shared company. A simple coffee break evolves into an extraordinary experience.

RETURNING TO TORONTO

I am returning to Toronto after nine months. And, having learned many things through many trials and even more errors, I feel like I am being given a second chance to connect with my adult daughter. Spending time with Maya in person has never felt like a test before. Mid-flight, I jot down a reminder in my notepad: *I control my narrative.* This is my chance to show Maya how I've evolved. I add a favourite Buddhist quote about speaking with kindness. "I am ready," I whisper to myself. I am still feeling weary from falling ill two weeks before the trip, from the intense planning. I feel the fragile weight of my aging body. I pray that there will be no accidents with my wheelchair, as there were on my previous journey east.

I close my eyes, hoping to steal a few moments of rest. By the time I finally get out of Toronto Pearson Airport and catch a wheelchair-accessible taxi to my hotel downtown, it is already 8:30 PM and the sun is setting. The sky is changing from soft pink to deep reddish purple, a symphony of colour welcoming me to the city and a restful evening. It is so spectacular, I briefly think of calling Maya, telling her to look up at the sky. But I think the better of it. I feel content to savour the anticipation of seeing her.

The next evening, I have dinner with Maya, as she is busy during the day. She chooses a Japanese restaurant conveniently situated between her new apartment and my hotel, just a ten-minute walk away. She comes to pick me up at the hotel lobby. While waiting, I can hardly contain my excitement. She is wearing the attire I remember so well: a beige cardigan and pants, a T-shirt, and a navy-blue lanyard with the U of T logo around her neck. Her favourite large white cotton tote hangs from her shoulder. Everything is familiar to me; she hasn't updated her wardrobe. The well-worn T-shirt she is wearing is one of the original Vancouver Arts Colloquium Society's shirts I designed a few years back. I realize that her choice is deliberate and thoughtful, which makes me feel so close to her. "Maya! It's wonderful to see you!" I cry and hug her tightly.

At the Japanese restaurant, we sit across from each other at a small table. While looking at the menu and deciding what to order, my nose itches and tears begin to well. "Ahhh, I'm just remembering how many times we used to do exactly this," I say, adding, "*Natsukashii!*" (So nostalgic!). Maya gives me a gentle smile. I hope I am not being too dramatic, but I can't help it. She orders avocado salad and California rolls, while I opt for agedashi tofu and udon, craving something warm to combat the chilly Toronto weather. Despite her familiar look, I notice something different in her—a newfound confidence and enthusiasm. She is fully present, making eye contact, unlike before when she used to avoid my gaze. She shares updates about her university life: that she has maintained a 4.0 GPA in her first year; that she is applying for neuroscience as her major; that she has accepted a paid internship; that she has started the new season of her choir club; that she has found new friends at U of T;

and, finally, that she has settled into her new condo with her boyfriend, Micah. We decide to surprise my father in Japan with a video call. Maya speaks very polite Japanese with him, and he seems overjoyed. She suddenly looks so grown-up. After dinner, she walks me back to my hotel, as if our roles have reversed. Concerned for her safety walking back alone in the big city after dark, I say goodbye at the intersection. Waving goodnight, I am grateful for her independence and maturity, but I am also aware of this new boundary between us, these divergent paths. I wish I could follow her across the crosswalk, but the red light reminds me to stay still.

The following two days, including Mother's Day, I get to spend time solely with Maya. Micah is out of town, and my accompanying friend, Jin, thoughtfully leaves us to ourselves. Our first destination is her new condo on Toronto's most iconic street, Yonge Street. With a small suitcase full of mementos and housewarming gifts, we arrive at her place; it is small but well set up and bright. She makes us tea and shows me every corner, even inside the drawers.

As we sit at the table, I keep looking around the tastefully decorated, modern interior. I notice a water jar on the kitchen counter with a small amount of white, murky liquid. "What is it, Maya?"

"Oh, it's lemon water, but the jar is too big to fit into the fridge," she replies, sipping her tea.

I continue, "You know, at room temperature, it may grow germs over time. I wouldn't drink that."

Silence. I notice a slight change in her facial expression. Sounding annoyed, she replies, "It's all taken care of."

I realize I have crossed a boundary, recalling similar exchanges with my own mother who used to check up on me and offer unsolicited advice. As I touch the dark-blue tablecloth with its Japanese print, I notice the marks of food spills. They must have been there for weeks, I think. Maya notices at the same time. This time, she gently says, "I have to wash this soon."

With smiles, I reply, "It's a beautiful tablecloth." I can empathize with her completely, as I recall my own youth when I often pushed back against my mother's one-sided approach. I say, "Is there anything I can do to make your life easier? Anything you need to buy? I'm only with you for a short time, so please let me know." These are words, I realize, that my own mother would have said.

For the rest of our time together we shop for clothes for Maya and Micah; visit the Japan Foundation Toronto Library (where I donate my book); explore the remarkable *From Edo to Meiji* exhibition of Japanese ceramics at the Royal Ontario Museum—its first public showing; have lunch and a coffee break; ride a streetcar (for the first time); and visit the Art Gallery of Ontario just like we did the last time. Returning to the AGO, we are revisiting our safe, familiar space where we created fond memories and where I discovered a new side of her. As she already has a free pass issued for those under the age of twenty-five, I try to pay for one adult ticket. However, the person at the front desk looks at us, pauses, and smiles. "Actually, you can enter as her companion. So, it's free for you." He waives my thirty-dollar entrance fee. I don't know if it is a policy or just a random act of kindness, but I appreciate it.

As it is Mother's Day, the museum is packed with visitors and families. We first check the current exhibition, *Making Her Mark: A History of Women Artists in Europe, 1400–1800*. This will be the perfect for a mother–daughter bonding experience! We linger over a painting titled *A Vase of Flowers,* painted in 1689 by Rachel Ruysch, a Dutch painter. "Wow, I like her perspective," we both exclaim. I look at the painting again and say, "This is the exact world I want to be in!" and I know that Maya understands what I mean. Unlike other flower paintings, this one depicts many flowers in different stages of their life cycles, from bloom to decay, and does so harmoniously and dramatically.

The canvas centres on perfect white flowers illuminated by a gentle light while the wilted flowers that surround them are cast in shadow. In this painting, I see a representation of a woman's life cycle, and the beautiful dynamic of women supporting women, particularly the act of lifting up our young women. I see my mother, my grandmother, and so many of my cherished older female friends reflected in the imagery. There's an unspoken yet undeniable message about our purpose and place in life—the quiet resilience of hidden flowers reappearing. The radiant white flower evokes Maya in my mind, while I see a reflection of myself in the wilting sunflower at the base. Experiencing the wisdom of this painter alongside Maya brings me immense joy. It alone makes this entire trip worthwhile. Later, I learn that Rachel Ruysch was a mother of ten children and a professional still-life painter for almost seventy years. This was extremely rare in the seventeenth and eighteenth centuries, when women artists often stopped painting after marriage. She inspires me. This painting promises to be a key event in my navigation of empty-nest motherhood.

The next day marks another main attraction: my Toronto book launch. Unlike my previous launches in Vancouver, this one holds profound significance for me as Maya and Micah are attending a reading of mine for the first time. Although Maya has witnessed many of my public-speaking engagements in the past, this one is different. It is deeply personal. As I prepare for my talk, I weave in messages I want to share with her directly and indirectly, aware that this might be my only, possibly last, opportunity.

For the launch, I have chosen a small, independent bookstore called Flying Books. It is wheelchair accessible and conveniently located near my hotel. There are about twenty people in attendance, including some of my friends' friends from Toronto, as well as my new writer friend Cheuk Kwan, whom I met at the 2024 LiterASIAN Writers Festival. He brings along another accomplished writer, Lynne Kutsukake. Although my experience with writers' communities is somewhat limited, I've consistently observed a strong sense of mutual support rather than cutthroat competition.

I am surprised to find myself in my element, speaking in a calm yet passionate voice, and making eye contact with each member of the audience. Maya and Micah are seated in the front row, their eyes fixed on me. After speaking for about thirty minutes or so, I open the floor to questions from the audience. Micah poses several insightful ones. I happen to mention that the last chapter of my book was written by eleven-year-old Maya, a section that my publisher and editor loved. Then, I turn to Maya and impulsively say, "Maya, I wonder if you would be willing to read your essay... Sorry, I don't mean to put you on the spot." As I say this, I am already preparing to gracefully accept her refusal. She looks a bit puzzled, but without much hesitation, she replies, "Sure!" I grab my iPhone, eager not to miss a moment.

She turns to face the audience and begins to read in her clear and humble voice. The room falls silent as everyone becomes engrossed in her story. Although I have always known Maya to be a talented writer and speaker, this is the first time I have heard her read this essay aloud, an essay that I have read countless times and that always moves me to tears. As I listen, memories flood my mind. She hasn't simply been a part of my life's work, she's understood it, she's captured its heart, she's captured us—the community. I hold back tears and immerse myself in the moment. It is one of the most profound experiences of my life. It is her Mother's Day gift to me.

ODE TO JOY

"So lovely to be in your presence again even for such a brief time. I don't know if you realize what a radiant aura surrounds you. Peace. Gratitude. Vibrancy. Optimism. It's almost like a physical light," Joy writes in her email to me, after we reconnect at the twelfth annual LiterASIAN

Writers Festival in 2024. Both of us are invited authors, and seeing my profile photo next to the legendary Joy Kogawa's on the promotional poster feels surreal. After her performance at the festival, I approach her. As soon as our eyes meet, we hug. While holding my hand tight, Joy asks a staff member to bring me one of the two large flower bouquets she received at her lifetime achievement ceremony. I can still feel the warmth of her delicate, gentle hand. Throughout the festival, I feel as though I am in a dream. Everything is a new experience for me as a first-time author. I had never even imagined that I would become a writer. It's like being swept onto a Noh stage, surprising everyone, including myself.

I met Joy in the spring of 2014, exactly ten years ago, at a book launch at the Historic Joy Kogawa House in Vancouver. We quickly bonded, and I learned about her fierce passion for addressing climate change, particularly her views on nuclear energy. True to her vision of being "not anti-nuclear," Joy proposed a series of small group meetings titled *Dialogue about How to Dialogue* around the issue. She reached out to me and Olivia Fermi, a granddaughter of Enrico Fermi (the Italian-born American Nobel Prize-winning physicist known as the creator of the world's first artificial nuclear reactor), to serve as organizers. At that time, I knew little about nuclear energy and had no experience organizing groups. Despite that, out of pure curiosity, I jumped in. Joy also contacted prominent physicists Patrick Walden and Anne Trudel from TRIUMF, Canada's particle accelerator centre. She also invited her lifelong friend and confidant Allan Davison, a professor in the Department of Biomedical Physiology and Kinesiology at Simon Fraser University, with whom I later became close friends. The six of us—Joy, Olivia, Patrick, Anne, Allan, and myself—met several times, including for discussions at my house, where we used a herring-bone graphic tool to explore both pro- and anti-perspectives, making the complexity accessible. We even took a field trip to see the film *Pandora's Promise*, a documentary about the nuclear power debate. Later, I helped arrange a meeting with my friend Constance Barnes, a former Vancouver Park Board Commissioner who is advocating for arts and culture amid her NDP nomination campaign. Together with Joy, Olivia, and Maureen from Canada's Citizens' Climate Lobby (CCCL), we gathered to discuss our shared interests. While the in-person dialogue series ended before yielding a specific tangible conclusion, I learned a great deal about how nuclear energy could evoke strong emotional reactions on both sides and the importance of having a conversation.

Among the many email correspondences between Joy, Olivia, and me, one message from Joy remains close to my heart:

> The book I have been writing, *Gently to Nagasaki*, comes out of the pressure cooker you describe, the holding of the contradictions. You have probably come across *The Bells of Nagasaki* by Takashi Nagai, a nuclear physicist who was there when the bomb fell. The book is in part a trek to the heart of mercy in his life. And to the friend within the enemy. I am expecting to hear within weeks

whether the work will see print. In a word, my walk is one of trust. In my experience, trust is an antidote to a contagion of fear.

She often emphasizes how emotion trumps logic and the importance of including "an appeal to what we feel." My respect and affection for Joy grows with every exchange.

Since then, Joy and I, despite her busy schedule, have grown closer through Japanese dinner parties and numerous email exchanges. She is always keen on making connections for others and has introduced me to many of her contacts, and this has led to fruitful collaborations and new friendships. Just over a year after we met in 2014, I began to feel as if she were my Vancouver mother. In the spring of 2015, she wrote in an email, "You are one of my reasons for wanting to come back to live in Vancouver. I'll see how it is to be in Toronto again. It's been such a long time. Most of the time in Vancouver, I've been quite isolated, which is what happens when I'm working hard."

Often after I send out a newsletter for my non-profit organization, she will send me a short line that relates show proud she is of me. Her words hold a profound significance for me and draws me into her beautiful world of love, trust, and kindness.

During the Covid pandemic, Joy's closest friend, Allan, joined in an intergenerational Zoom meet-up that I had organized as part of my non-profit activities. The intent of the meeting was to discuss the blending of art and science.

Additionally, Allan and I collaborated to record a series called *The Correspondence* on conversations covering a range of topics. In one of these conversations, Allan shared his previous discussion with Joy on how easy it is to make friends, but how difficult it is to judge a person's character, and how little time it takes before you decide if someone can actually *be* your friend. Allan recalled, "Joy said it is actually about three minutes." We both chuckled before he continued, "I thought that's true for me as well, because people are open and present themselves genuinely as who they really are. That alone is enough."

Reflecting on this, I wonder if my deep connections with Joy and Allan were set in our first three minutes of encounter; this made me feel that fate was at work. Despite the thirty-two-year age difference between myself and them, I always feel that I can talk about anything without being judged and that I can easily connect. This ease of communication is a result of their honourable and humble natures. When I remarked on Allan's compassionate way with words, he credits Joy, from whom he learned to be open-minded and kind. Birds of a feather.

During the 2024 LiterASIAN Writers Festival, Joy informed me that Allan had opted for Medical Assistance in Dying (MAID) a couple of months earlier. He was eighty-eight years old. I was shocked and saddened, realizing I hadn't had the chance to say thank you and goodbye. The last time I heard from him was about six months prior, when he had sent me a congratulatory message on my book launch. Our phone conversations had become scarce as I became occupied with my own affairs. After our last phone conversation, he wrote to me expressing his empathy and noting the loss he felt in my voice regarding my sorrow that I could no longer wake up with my daughter in the house. He was empathetic, as always.

Immediately following the 2024 LiterASIAN Writers Festival, I travelled to Toronto for another book reading and the chance to see Maya, and possibly Joy, as she was also returning to Toronto at that time. She graciously connected me with contacts at the Japanese Canadian Cultural Centre, who generously offered me a tour. She even arranged for me to be interviewed by *Nikkei Voice*, the Japanese-Canadian national newspaper, ahead of my Toronto book launch. On my final day in Toronto we met for lunch at a restaurant called Eatery. Concerned that my choice of meeting location might be inconvenient for her, I offered to arrange a taxi. However, she insisted on taking the subway, noting that it would be good for her brain to break from routine.

She arrived dressed in a tan linen jacket, a cream-coloured silk scarf inherited from her mother, white gloves, and a baseball cap on her signature short white hair. She looked so elegant and pure, like a lily. And keen-eyed, too, like a curious young girl. Once, I sent her a photo of my late maternal grandmother, Tamiko. Joy reminded me of her with her kind eyes and humble demeanour. Joy took one look at it and exclaimed, "Good heavens, she's my doppelgänger!"

Over salad and pizza, we raised our glasses to our beloved Allan. Joy said, "When we remember people we love, even though they are no longer here, they are actually with us. We are connected." She looked up, smiling sweetly, as if Allan were joining us from above. I followed her gesture, looked up, and smiled. While savouring the delicious meal, she said she would like to return to this restaurant alone, to again enjoy the pizza and break her routine. She seemed so comfortable and happy in this trendy, busy restaurant, which made me happy. We talked about shared memories, our families, her life in Toronto, and mysterious dreams we both had the previous night. She brought me her homemade *nishime*, a traditional Japanese dish of cooked mushrooms. I found it too precious to eat and that brought tears to my eyes. I felt an overflowing love, as if she and my grandmother Tamiko had melted together.

Joy also informed me about the upcoming opening of the WongAvery Asia Pacific Peace Museum in Toronto in June 2024, for which she wrote the opening statement. This first-of-its-kind museum is dedicated to educating people about the atrocities the Japanese perpetuated in Asia during the Second World War. It aims to foster reconciliation and peace. True to her strong conviction that trust and truth free us, she said, “We are descendants of Japan and cannot run away and hide.”

Two hours flew by quickly, and it was time to head back. Joy, full of energy, said she wanted to walk home, and that it would probably take an hour or so. I was impressed by her spirit but worried about her navigating the busy and crowded streets. We started down Yonge Street together. She looked at me with gentle eyes and said, “I love you.”

I replied, “I love you too, Joy,” my own eyes brimming with tears.

The day was warm and muggy and after walking for about twenty minutes, she decided to take the subway. We hugged and looked into each other's eyes as I promised to return to Toronto to see her again. Her word, "connected," stays with me.

THE SPIDER AND I

I am going through my ritual preparations for bed when I spot the massive spider nestled in the curve of my bathroom sink. I gasp. My eyes fix on her. I don't know why, but I assume it is female. She is about ten centimetres in diameter. I freeze. She freezes also, but I sense her vitality. Her eight legs are spread wide, as if poised to strike. Despite my fear of spiders, I cautiously navigate my wheelchair around the occupied sink and prepare to use the other one, the one where my daughter used to brush her teeth when she lived with me.

I resist the urge to flee; I had seen a similar creature two months ago in the same spot. I screamed and jolted. That spider occupied my sink for three consecutive days until my handyman, Vincent, compassionately caught her and released her outside.

This time it is late evening, and I have no one to call for help. A chilling thought: can the spider sense my rising fear? "Pumpkin!" I call my cat in a panicked voice, hoping for some moral support, if not actual pest control. Trying to retreat into normalcy, I swiftly brush my teeth and wash my face. While wiping my face with a towel, I glance at the occupied sink. Again, I am shocked; the spider is gone. Without moving, I cautiously survey my surroundings, searching for her. She is nowhere to be seen. I slowly approach the occupied sink, and I spot her on the other side of the sink's curve.

Did she just move to that side to hide, I wonder. If so, how intelligent she must be. I feel a strange connection to her, as if we are playing hide-and-seek. I conjure an image of our initial meeting a few minutes before, her numerous eyes—perhaps all eight, perhaps only a few—seeming to briefly connect with mine. Then, she observes me patiently until the perfect moment comes to quickly hide.

Why does such a large spider keep returning to my bathroom sink, especially to the same, exact spot? There are five identical sinks upstairs. Why this one? Do spiders have preferences? Does she want to be seen by me or play with me? These wild questions linger.

Then I recall a similar encounter with a large spider in my grandparents' bathroom, back when I was a child. My grandparents often referred to large spiders as protectors of the house and holders of wisdom. A comforting thought rises that perhaps this spider, too, has some personal connection, a message from beyond. The realization settles in that, despite the quiet of my empty nest these past twelve months, I am not alone. My house holds other lives. Could this spider be a symbolic presence? Is she a reincarnation of my grandmother? Almost unconsciously, I whisper, "My relations." To my surprise, my fear subsides. We humans naturally create such stories to cope with fear and to ensure our survival.

I watch her from a safe remove. Even from a distance, her grotesque appearance sends a shiver down my spine, yet a deeper feeling emerges: a sense of almost tender reverence. The experience transcends the purely physical; it is both spiritual and aesthetic. As I pass by the sink to turn off the bathroom light, I gently say, "Good night."

I lie in bed, but my mind is still on the spider. Remembering how the previous spider had stayed in the same spot for three days, I knew I'd see her there again tomorrow morning. Unlike my initial reaction to such a large spider two months ago, I feel a different connection this time. I sense character, spirit, and a strange beauty beneath her fearsome appearance. What changed my way of looking?

I find her there again the next morning, in the same spot, her legs tucked close to her body, making her seem smaller, less threatening. "Good morning," I murmur, expecting that she is still asleep. The thought of using my daughter's sink with its awkward drawers fills me with some discomfort. It means manoeuvring my wheelchair sideways and twisting my body in an uncomfortable way just to wash my face. I wonder, with a touch of resignation, how long this will go on—how long this spider will occupy my accessible space?

That day, I have a lovely weekend lunch with my German friends, Daniel and Ela, at my home. During our nearly five-hour conversation, I happen to mention the spider upstairs, describing how large it is. Daniel and Ela offer to remove her from my sink and release her outside. They are both nature lovers. I gratefully accept, feeling slightly guilty. Ela deftly captures the spider. She tells me that as soon as the spider saw her, it started circling inside the sink. She swiftly placed a glass jar over it and then slid a sheet of paper underneath.

They release the spider into the garden.

Strangely, I am both relieved and guilt-struck. Should I have waited for her to leave on her own? What if she is my grandmother's reincarnation? What stories might we have woven together? The novel *Life of Pi*, by Yann Martel, comes to mind. In that novel, an Indian boy named Pi survives a shipwreck and finds himself adrift in the Pacific Ocean on a lifeboat with a tiger and other animals. The spider reminds me of the tiger on the lifeboat, a vital focus that needs to feel alive and to survive in the uncertain world. Pi, alone on the boat, could have easily been buried by despair and lost the will to live. Sometimes, I feel similarly overwhelmed by loneliness and solitude, especially on quiet evenings. That spider reminds me of the interconnectedness of the world around me, transcending time.

There's a Japanese saying: "What happens twice happens three times." I feel that I will see her again in a couple of months or so.

I am not surprised when another spider appears one evening, this time at the base of the tall bathroom window. Slightly smaller, but still unsettlingly large, I know it isn't the same one as before. Perhaps one of its young? I am relieved by the distance between the window and the sink. While brushing my teeth, I can't resist glancing over. She remains perfectly still, as if deep in contemplation. But the moment I turn to rinse, she vanishes, as if swallowed by the shadows. Ha! It seems our little game of hide-and-seek has resumed.

Each evening, she materializes in her usual spot, keeping me company for a short while before vanishing into the depths. It appears she is lingering, waiting for my customary "Good night." Every night, as I head toward my bathroom, I now expect to see her. It becomes a nightly ritual. "Good evening! How was your day? Perhaps yours is just beginning!" I say, half-expecting a response. I observe her suspended in her intricate web, woven into the bottom corner of the window, and wonder if this aerial perch offers the perfect view of her domain.

Driven by my growing fascination, I research the sensory world of spiders. I learn they have no ears in the human sense but rather detect vibrations through highly sensitive nerve-based receptors on their legs. This revelation prompts me to consider how the vibrations of my electric toothbrush, coupled with the harsh glare and buzzing hum of the bathroom light might impact her. Oh, well. Her consistent reappearance in the same spot suggests a shared, albeit unspoken, understanding of our shared space and daily routines. I even notice her moving gracefully into the cabinet's base—a sign, perhaps, of mutual comfort. Has she simply gone to bed before me?

On many evenings, her presence conjures a comforting image: my grandmother, returned in this unexpected form, watching over me and whispering bedtime stories as she did during my childhood. I offer my spider a smile and a quiet "Thank you, goodnight" in Japanese. As the bathroom light clicks off, the darkness that envelopes the room feels palpable, almost like it's breathing, and for some reason I think of the delicate threads of her web as she first begins to spin them.

One night I enter the bathroom to prepare for bed and I am immediately struck by her absence. I gasp, unease seizing me. Has she died? Has she found a better spot? Has she not found enough to eat in this winter? I feel empty, as if I have lost a companion. She is gone. A week later, my eye catches a small, dark, curled-up form against my white bedroom carpet. It looks like a desiccated insect. It takes a day or two for the realization to dawn: it is her. I've been avoiding it, hoping my cat, Pumpkin, would investigate, or that my cleaning lady would vacuum it up. I can't bring myself to touch it. But now the truth is undeniable.

Why had she chosen my bedroom to die? Perhaps it was simply the quietest corner of the house, a peaceful place to rest. Or perhaps, in some way I can't understand she felt a connection to me, to the space I occupied. I gently scoop her up with a piece of paper and place her outside under a sweet box bush. "My relations," I whisper again, this time with a sense of finality. As I water the flowers, I think of my grandmother, of the stories she used to tell. I realize that the spider, in her own way, has told me a story, too—a story of quiet companionship in a lonely time.

The bathroom feels empty. And I have changed.

PATCHWORK

I cannot keep putting it off: I need a haircut. A friend of mine recommends Gideon, her hair stylist. Serendipity! He apparently lives just a few blocks away and, even better, makes house calls for very special clients. How is it possible that I've lived in this neighbourhood for over fourteen years, and I've never even heard of him? I immediately schedule an appointment and now eagerly anticipate the day.

Gideon is a character. He is a married man in his late fifties, with a grown daughter and a truly independent spirit. His towering presence is softened by a warm smile and a kilt—yes, a kilt—that he proudly wears year-round in homage to his Irish heritage. But his talents extend beyond hairdressing. He is renowned as an oil painter and has apparently graced the pages of a Canadian art history book.

Gideon is also a budding scientist and experiments with hydroponics at home. And he is a skilled chef, his love for food growing out of his scientific curiosity. "One thing's for sure," he chuckles, snipping away at my hair, "I'll never be bored."

As a natural storyteller, Gideon exudes a vitality that is infectious. He possesses a keen observational eye and an endless curiosity. When I ask his secret to a fulfilling later life, he simply replies, "Be the person you want to meet and spend time with."

My hair now graces my shoulders in a chic, short bob.

Unexpected gifts start appearing on my doorstep: homemade popcorn, fresh coleslaw, beef chilli, and even a kind offer to sharpen my kitchen knives. Gideon is more than a neighbour; he is a friend gifted with abundant humanity and generosity. He says, “I like to surprise you. I like to see you smile,” adding, “I think you are very beautiful. Sorry if that is too forward.”

Blushing at the unexpected compliment, I wonder if he might be fond of me. But his gentle nature and quirky charm put me at ease.

Then I discover his passion for board games, and his collection of over three hundred of them! “Would you be free on Tuesday or Wednesday for a little cooking and a nice quiet board game?” texts Gideon. Our shared curiosity and openness for new experiences lead to weekly board game nights where he also shows off impressive culinary skills. From the rich depth of his beef barley soup to his delicately balanced Singapore egg-drop crab laksa, each dish highlights his creative nature. The shared meals enhance our bond, bestowing laughter, warm conversation, and camaraderie.

Each week brings new gaming challenges as Gideon samples his vast collection. A novice to the world of board games, I am initially overwhelmed by the rules and strategies. I have a competitive nature that must be able to meet a challenge.

Gideon’s wisdom always impresses me. When I exclaim, “I won!” during our board game nights, he calmly responds, “It’s the journey, not the destination.”

One evening, during a game of Patchwork, a shift occurs. For the first time, I feel detached from the outcome. Perhaps it is the game's emphasis on chance rather than strategy, as Gideon explains. Regardless, I experience a newfound sense of tranquility. While the game still presents challenges and requires sacrifices, it still offers multiple chances and opportunities. Gideon quietly says, "I don't have attachments in life. It's full of surprises."

That night, as the game concludes, I can't shake the feeling that something profound has shifted. Gideon's philosophy of non-attachment resonates deeply with Zeami's hidden flowers. His delight in surprising others, his insightful observations, and his generosity, coupled with his understanding of non-attachment, seem to unlock the secret to constantly discovering beauty in unexpected places. I am relishing this newfound awareness when I get an abrupt interruption: a text from Shu. We hadn't seen each other for six months.

Shu writes, "I meant to ask you. I don't know how you're feeling about us since we haven't seen each other for a while, but I would be happy to keep seeing you intimately from time to time if you feel the same way. I crave your physical contact and touch and our fun conversations." The stark difference between his suggestion and my yearning for emotional connection brings an unanticipated clarity of thought. While the decision to end that chapter is sad and disappointing, I now understand it is a necessary step, a crucial act of self-care to honour my own emotional well-being.

I reply, "I really like you, but it is difficult for me to separate intimacy and emotion. I want to be with someone who can be emotionally involved. I hope to remain as your good friend." I am calm as I write.

He replies, "It saddens me that we won't see each other in this way anymore. I really miss our time together. I will always cherish our memories made together."

As I accept our farewell, I feel a sense of peace along with a sense of relief and a renewed focus on myself.

This experience with Shu has been a game with unexpected twists and turns. Could a kiss without attachment be worthwhile? Perhaps. It entirely depends on one's current values and priorities. Life takes unpredictable turns, but we can savour each moment. While the ending is certain, the expedition is ours to enjoy.

Lying in bed, I replay the game of Patchwork. The thrill of anticipation, the rewards of patience, and the simple joy of the present moment fill my mind. Every relationship has its own set of rules. And like a mindful player, I choose to play with heart and strength, but without the tether of attachment.

My friendship with Shu continues with sporadic exchanges of texts and photos. One day, Shu calls me to ask if I'd be interested in trying a float house sensory deprivation experience in Epsom salt water. "Would you help me in?" I ask.

"Of course, that's the idea. It might be a new experience for you. I'm interested in trying it and thought you might enjoy it too," he replies. I chuckle, recognizing this offer as typical of his adventurous spirit, another token being added to our final round of Patchwork, whether realized or remaining.

Two months later, Shu takes a job on the East Coast and begins packing. We are all playing our ongoing game of Patchwork, a fitting metaphor for life's give and take. *Fin de partie*!

COUNTRY ROADS

I bought a cheap guitar in the early summer of 2024 to teach myself how to play. Perhaps I was seeking something new, or maybe I was trying to move past my wishful thinking that Maya might return over summer break. But I was also thinking of my late uncle Tetsurō, who played guitar in his youth and then restarted playing in his seventies. Perhaps I was imitating him to tap into a kind of fulfillment I had yet to discover.

Now, I set a goal to master one song to sing at my annual Christmas party, giving myself about six months to practice. While searching Japanese YouTube for an easy arrangement, I come across "Take Me Home, Country Roads," a 1971 John Denver song that holds a special place in Japanese hearts thanks to Yoko Honna's cover and its use in the beloved Studio Ghibli film *Whisper of the Heart*. The arrangement has only four notes: D, A, G, and C. It seems manageable, even though I have never played the guitar before. However, once I start practicing, I find

TAKE ME HOME
watercolour,
9 × 12

The song "Take Me Home, Country Roads" holds a special place in my heart. It evokes memories of childhood summers spent driving through lush green farmlands on the way to Mount Aso, the windows down, and the wind in my hair. Even though those roads may have changed, I can always return to that feeling in my memory.

that pressing the correct strings with my left hand is more difficult than I imagined, especially the C chord.

Despite my frustratingly slow progress, I enjoy playing the catchy part of the song, especially with the Japanese lyrics. I find them deeply moving, and their expression feels distinct from the American original, adding a satisfying twist.

I love these lyrics as they express a yearning for home that dovetails with my own experience. The phrase (my translation) "Even if this road continues to my hometown, I'm not going. I can't go to the country road" brings me to tears. The words encapsulate the complexities of my wheelchair and of my frail physical health and lead me to consider how these challenges have kept me from Japan for the last eighteen years. They express my sacrifice of missed experiences and cherished memories.

I think about why I have chosen these sacrifices. Can I still cry from homesickness after all I've endured? Even when confined to my wheelchair, I know I must forge a life in Vancouver that justifies my choices. I can't waste my investment on the past. Singing along to "I can't go to the country road," I also realize that I am afraid of triggering my homesickness and my subliminal desire to leave Vancouver. The song perfectly crystallizes my sentiments.

Meanwhile, our family LINE group has been quite active, mostly with communication between my sister and my father as they discuss the details of the new family home design and prepare for his temporary move during the construction. I've become less involved in the house project, though I occasionally suggest wheelchair-accessible designs, which my sister kindly supports. The family home recedes into the distance as the days go by.

Am I feeling left out? Do I still resent my father? Certainly not anymore. But I realize I am still intensely homesick, a feeling I can't afford to indulge.

I never imagined that our family house in Kumamoto—the one I will never live in again—would become a source of longing. It isn't so much the house I am missing; it is my family in Japan. The intense LINE exchanges that include photos from their family vacations and numerous family gatherings are a paradox to me: connection and disconnection, closeness and distance, insiders and outsiders, joy and sorrow.

"Grow up, Keiko," my inner voice says. I know what I need to do now. As my father is almost eighty-eight years old, I want to convey nothing but joy, gratitude, and honour in every exchange I have with him. I know I need organize myself to travel to Japan to see my family next year when the wheelchair-accessible house will be ready.

Later that summer, I am pulled back to Kumamoto in a most unexpected way. In early March 2023, Yasuhiro, a friend from my high school days who is now a Japanese corporate executive stationed in Colombia, unexpectedly contacted me to join the Kumamoto high school's LINE group, a group I have unintentionally avoided for years. I found myself wondering why I had stayed away for so long. Perhaps my avoidance was due to a combination of my introverted nature and the feeling of being an outsider to Japanese social circles.

Yasuhiro also reached out to another classmate, Tomo, now an engineering professor at a US university, and created a separate three-person LINE group for us, aptly named The Americas. The name felt particularly fitting for this unique and geographically dispersed reunion.

Nearly four decades have passed since our high school graduation, and I haven't seen them since. Yasuhiro's invitation sent my heart racing. It was a chance for adventure, a chance to reconnect with my past—or maybe with my future.

I wondered if this reconnection was a message from Kumamoto, a signal from some strange, internal compass. In our age of constant digital connection, the timing felt poetic. Perhaps there was more to these coincidences.

A constant thread of connection and reconnection runs throughout the year, woven from frequent texts and shared photos. We exchange updates on work and family and, sometimes, on books we are reading or quotes that inspire us. As seasoned travellers, they often send photo from their personal and business trips, each image accompanied by cultural and historical details that bring the places they visit to life. It's as if I am travelling with them—New York, Washington, DC, Portugal, Spain, Germany, and, of course, Japan.

At last, in the summer of 2024, the first in-person reunion of The Americas becomes a reality in Vancouver. Yasuhiro makes the long journey from Bogotá, and Tomo flies from Virginia, all for a precious few days together. Thanks to their incredible efforts, it feels as though the very spirit of Kumamoto, carried on the familiar melody of "Country Roads," has miraculously bridged time and space to be with me. I silently offer my gratitude for the extraordinary fortune of having such wonderful, capable, and compassionate friends. It's a truly remarkable story.

In the days leading up to the reunion, sleep eludes me, not only due to sheer excitement but also because of the flurry of preparations for my special guests. To commemorate our long-awaited reunion, I even design and create T-shirts featuring the world-famous Kumamon mascot—the wide-eyed, red-cheeked bear created by the Kumamoto Prefectural government. I suggest we all wear them while kayaking in False Creek, and Yasuhiro and Tomo sweetly agree. We would truly look like the Three Amigos, a sight to behold.

My Vancouver home becomes a portal to the past during those precious few days. We relive the magic of our high school years, our late nights filled with laughter and stories, the aroma of shared meals mingling with Tomo's impromptu piano playing, all set against the backdrop of a beautiful, pleasantly cool, long Vancouver summer day. Some of my Vancouver friends who know about the reunion offer encouragement, food, and support. Musqueam weaver Debra Sparrow meets us at Musqueam Village and shares the historical timeline of how the Coast Salish met the Spanish in the 1790s and then gifts us with a smoked salmon. What a warm welcome! We visit the Museum of Anthropology, the Beaty Biodiversity Museum, Kits Beach, and Stanley Park—the best of Vancouver. We even manage to create *yosegaki*, those beautiful Japanese collaborative message boards, for each of us to take home as a memento of our reunion.

It is a dream, a reunion I never truly believed would happen. What a joy to be with these two wonderful childhood friends who share the same roots, the same formative experiences as I do. I'm incredibly proud of their hard-won achievements; they've surpassed anything I could have imagined. They are truly the best in their respective fields, though their extraordinary talents were already evident in their academic and athletic achievements back then. It is a strangely wonderful feeling, but I feel I am back in Kumamoto, back in high school in their presence. It's like we're those same kids again, full of dreams and innocence, and a touch of mystery.

Kumamoto isn't so far away after all. "Country Roads" means something different to me now. I will replace the lyrics with: "Even if this road does not continue to my hometown, I'm going . . . one day."

MONO NO AWARE (物の哀れ)

One Sunday afternoon, I am sipping tea in my living room with my new friend Andy. Andy is a soft-spoken artist in his thirties. Like my daughter, he's half-Japanese and half-Caucasian. I met him at a museum-led community forum and felt an immediate, inexplicable connection, almost like a kinship. He seemed to embody the contradictions of Japan—orderly yet enigmatic, elegant yet complex. His relaxed voice contrasted with his carefully chosen and sophisticated words in a way that fascinates me.

We explore together the subtle ways our Japanese heritage influences our daily lives, often surprising us with just how "Japanese" we are. "I'm drawn to places that are dimly lit, both physically and figuratively," Andy says with a chuckle. It makes me think of Tanizaki's *In Praise of Shadows*, first published in 1933, a beautiful exploration of how traditional Japanese aesthetics value the nuances of darkness. I chime in, "We Japanese embrace darkness as a productive element."

He astutely observes that his seventy-year-old mother lights up when she shifts from English to Japanese. This makes me wonder how my own character or demeanour might shift depending on the language I speak. He also shares that she is gradually losing her English vocabulary—a common occurrence with aging that I certainly can relate to. Understanding the importance of her connection to her heritage, he is about to embark on a two-week trip to Japan with her, a journey of both cultural and familial significance.

"Wow, you're an amazing son, Andy," I say, impressed by his thoughtful nature and maturity.

"Well, when I was young, she had a tough time with me," he adds, "but I love my mother dearly."

Smiling, I reply, "Have you ever shared your concerns with her that she is losing her English vocabulary?"

"No, I haven't. She would just laugh," he says.

Andy's keen observation and caring ways remind me of the Japanese way of looking for shadows where the beauty is often hidden. Perhaps it is *saga*—something ingrained? Who knows. Before becoming an architect, Andy aspired to be a physical and occupational therapist, often volunteering to work with people with disabilities. His inclination to seek out dimly lit places in the world is uniquely his, not necessarily cultural, yet he described it earlier as a Japanese trait. He also mentions his ongoing confusion about his cultural identity, acknowledging that he doesn't feel fully Japanese or fully Canadian, or anything in between. I wonder about Maya and if she will similarly find herself in Andy's position one day, seeking identity in the half-spaces.

He asks me a series of intriguing questions, such as, "To what extent has Maya been exposed to Japanese culture? Do you think it will influence her sense of identity?"

I reply, "That's a good question. But I'd say no, because she didn't grow up in Japan and has no direct memories of the land, unlike me." I explain that my Japanese identity is deeply connected to specific sensory experiences that are unique to Japan, like waking up to loud cicadas in summer; smelling the incense my grandmother burned every morning to worship our ancestors; and listening to the soothing sounds of crickets on tranquil autumn nights while studying for my exams. I can easily remember the smell of moist earth that hits me as soon as I land at Narita Airport. It's such a Japanese smell, and it always means I am home.

"However, I'm certain her Japanese identity will be strongly connected to her relationship with my mother," I continue. "My mother cherished Maya and they shared baths, dance, and laughter together. That's a bodily memory."

Andy chimes in. "For me, I am taken back when I hear the sound of bundled chopsticks being washed. My mother did it by holding her hands together and moving like this." He demonstrates the Japanese praying gesture by rubbing his hands together.

I exclaim, "My grandmother did the same thing to wash chopsticks, and the sound is so familiar to me too!" A strange sensation seizes me, as if I am reminiscing about family memories with relatives. As Tanizaki might say, these seemingly small details are crucial to understanding Japanese culture, engaging all the senses.

He asks me if I would consider returning to Japan, perhaps thinking of his mother who regretted giving up her Japanese citizenship after experiencing intense homesickness. I sigh and reply, "Well, in my case, I have no choice but to stay here, even though I'm still a Japanese citizen. Due to climate change, Japan is becoming increasingly uninhabitable during the summer. Since I can't sweat because of my injury, it's a matter of life and death. Plus, I can't imagine how I would fit into the conformist culture after decades of living overseas," I add, "I'm making my home here."

We continue chatting about various topics, including must-watch films. We agree that we want to rewatch

Perfect Days, my now-favourite film. He says, "Next Monday, I'm going to see a Japanese film, *Living in Two Worlds,* about the relationship between a son and his deaf mother. I can't help but be drawn to such stories, especially those involving mothers. If you're free, we can watch it together."

I wonder what new perspectives I might gain through his unique lens as the son of a Japanese mother from Japan. I think of Maya and Andy, their lives and perspectives overlapping in my mind.

My shy cat, Pumpkin, leaps up on the table, signalling that it is time to wrap up our afternoon gathering.

The following week, the theatre is packed with eager audiences for the film *Living in Two Worlds*. From a distance, I notice Andy waving his hand and smiling. From the beginning of the film, he is moved to tears and sniffs softly, as does the woman sitting next to him. Soon, the entire theatre is filled with the sound of sniffling. For some reason, I work hard to hold back my sobs and to silently swallow my tears. Why? Is it Japanese stoicism, or simply moderation? The film resonates so deeply with my own experiences as both a mother and a daughter. My eyes continue to well up with tears. Andy reminds me of Maya. Watching this film about a mother with a disability and her son provides a perfect contemplative space, like a mirror reflecting the absence of my mother and my daughter, even as their shadows remain so deeply ingrained in my inner world.

"Wow. Let's unpack what we saw," Andy suggests after the film. His eyes are bloodshot and puffy under the natural light, likely mirroring my own. We find a table in a bustling mall cafeteria and revisit poignant scenes from the movie until my ride arrives.

In the cafeteria, the constant ebb and flow of people resembles a fast-forwarded film, perfectly capturing life's relentless forward momentum, and yet, familiar scenes seem to repeat. A flashback scene from the film haunts me. The protagonist, the son of a deaf mother, now an adult, recounts his teenage years with tears in his eyes. As a rebellious teen, he had accused her of being absent and useless during the times he needed her most. Those harsh words make me reflect on my own teenage experiences and my daughter's as well. With a mother confined to a wheelchair, she had to grow up quickly and in a different way from other children.

Andy identifies with the protagonist. His eyes again fill with tears as he shares his troubled youth and his mother's Japanese tendency to silence. I add, "Just like the deaf mother in the film, Japanese mothers don't need to hear words of apology or hugs from their adult children. They can perfectly sense your feelings just by looking at you. She understood." As I say this to him, I wonder if I am speaking to myself, or perhaps thinking of Maya, or even indirectly addressing her. My memory of my own mother surfaces, her gentle words after a tense argument: "*Daijōbu, genki wo dashinasai,*" meaning, "It's okay, be cheerful." Perhaps she, too, understood the unspoken apologies in my heart.

CHANGED AND UNCHANGED

Exactly one year ago today, August 28, 2023, we were packing the last items for Maya's move to Toronto. She had lived in this house for the last time. We finished dinner early and prepared for bed early as we had to wake at 2:00 AM to catch the 6:00 AM flight. A mix of emotions—happiness, anxiety, excitement, and grief—swirled through me. I tried to feel every moment, storing away memories of our shared home. Each glance at Maya filled me with tears. I was overwhelmed by the finality. We spoke mostly about practical matters; discussing our emotions was too painful.

The atmosphere of the house has changed significantly since Maya has left. It's now more relaxed, orderly, solitary, yet still joyful. A year ago, I could never have predicted this.

Around the time Maya finished her first year, a big change occurred. Maya and Micah moved into a condo together to share student life. At their initiative, our weekly Sunday Zoom calls became three-person Zoom calls. Adding Micah improved the dynamic between Maya and me. Every week, we discussed politics, books, films, their spontaneous discoveries in Toronto, and foods they were eating and cooking. They often recommended what to watch on Netflix, and then we discussed it afterward. We constructed a new ritual: at the end of each call, we took a screenshot of the three of us to chart our evolution.

Over the last year, Maya's face has gotten rounder and more radiant. She is now an adult woman. More interestingly, I started understanding Micah better. Rather than seeing him as my daughter's lover and protector, I started seeing him more as a kind of son or a close family member. That gradual shift changed the way I relate to Maya. I was no longer a person standing between Maya and Micah; rather, I was in their expanded circle.

One day, Maya texted me to ask if I could send her my meat sauce pasta recipe. It was a total surprise. I could not believe it at first as Maya used to tease me about my cooking skills. Since I do not follow strict recipes, most of my dishes have no precise names. Still, some, such as meat sauce pasta and curry rice, have been Maya's favourite since she was small. Elated, I created a fancy looking recipe sheet of my sauce complete with a photo of the pasta, taken years ago. The next day, Maya and Micah texted me with the picture of their recreation of my meat sauce pasta: "It is super yummy! And easy to make. The recipe worked great." I couldn't have asked for a better outcome.

The first year of empty-nest life was turbulent, but I eventually emerged from it. My new life requires navigating an interconnected system of relationships involving mother–daughter, father–daughter, romantic, and self. I wonder if my personal challenges are amplifying the effects of empty-nest syndrome, or if the transition itself was the primary contributing factor to my struggles.

Recognizing the power of writing to shape our understanding of the world and ourselves, I'm diligently documenting my own journey of transition. This exploration extends beyond the written word and into the realm of lived experience—painting, a surprising (and nerve-wracking!) Christmas party singing debut, collaborative art projects, learning guitar, nurturing friendships, enjoying board games, and even revisiting (for the second time) Haruki Murakami's *The City and Its Uncertain Walls*. I navigate this emerging world, driven by a search for meaning—and this search is the source of my personal agency, my evolving identity, and my newfound happiness.

While many things have changed since last August, certain precious things have remained constant. My frequent email exchanges with Lesley Nan, the headmistress and founder of the Family School in NYC, have provided a sense of grounding and consistently remind me of the most precious part of my life: Maya. She often sends me old photos of us with Maya, writing, "Do you remember this little one?" These reminders evoke shared sentiments and strengthen our bond. Lesley is more than a friend—she is a mother figure, a wise and influential mentor, and a true role model.

My next door neighbours, Mr. and Mrs. Tu, have been incredibly kind. Even after Maya left Vancouver last summer, ninety-two-year-old Mr. Tu would frequently call me to say, "My wife made some noodles for you and Maya. I'll be over in five minutes." Most recently, Mrs. Tu, despite her hip and mobility problems, made shrimp crackers and included a beautifully handwritten letter addressed to both me and Maya saying, "How are you doing? I miss Maya so much. Maya, will you be able to come back for Christmas? Please greet her on my behalf." Maya makes a lasting impression on many friends and neighbours, I realize.

Over the last decade, Katsu-san and Yoko-san have consistently shown their care for me, often bringing incredible seasonal Japanese homemade dishes to my door or warmly inviting me to their beautiful home whenever they have the opportunity. I remember once how Yoko-san, the mother of two daughters, shared her wisdom on parenting: "It's good to always show her (Maya) a sign that says, 'I'm on your side.'" Her words strike me deeply, and they are not just words for parenting. I feel these two are always on my side, and with them I feel understood and supported. It is a profound emotional anchor for me, a source of unconditional love.

For the past five growing seasons or so, Marcel, my trusted friend and urban farmer from Germany, has faithfully brought me and his customers fresh, locally grown produce. This year, his generosity extends even further: he offers to clear out the raised beds in my front yard, plant a variety of vegetables, and even water them weekly. In return for his kindness, I propose to prepare a meal to share with him on his delivery day, Thursday. He is a man of both boundless curiosity and deep compassion, always observing the world around him, helping others, and sharing his knowledge and experiences. He's become a valued sounding board. I hope I offer him similar support.

My friend, Jin, a fellow empty-nester and age-mate, consistently amazes me of her caring nature and remarkable independence. She has a way of making me feel completely at ease, like a nurturing sister. I wonder how much her ex-husband must miss her presence in his life, as she possesses an uncanny ability to provide precisely the support needed, like scratching an itch in exactly the right spot. This year, despite her demanding work schedule, she generously accompanied me on my trip to Toronto, providing invaluable support and companionship. I attribute the success of my trip in large part to her presence and assistance.

My long-time friend, Patrick, is also a constant source of support, always willing to help with anything from a simple check-in to a ride. This year, in two separate emergencies—one involving my own sudden fever, the other Pumpkin's unexpected illness—he immediately dropped everything to drive us to the doctor.

My young friend, Marvel, a bright student at UBC, frequently shares his insightful perspectives with me and attends my cultural salon or community projects whenever his demanding university schedule allows. He calls me "his Vancouver Mom," and I playfully respond by calling him "my adopted son." I feel immense pride in all his endeavours, just as I do for all my young student friends. I sincerely hope that I can be a source of encouragement and support for them, their steadfast cheerleader as they navigate their academic journeys and beyond.

There are countless other friends with whom, over the years, I have formed strong bonds based on mutual trust. Pondering on my pure luck, I am reminded of *The Pillow Book*, Section 171: "A Woman Living Alone." Sei Shōnagon, a Japanese author, poet, and court lady who served the Empress Teishi around the year 1000 during the middle Heian period, writes (my translation):

> A solitary woman's dwelling, wild and untended, with crumbling earthen walls. Even in the pond, weeds proliferate, and while the garden isn't entirely overtaken by mugwort, patches of green grass brave the sandy soil. It's the very loneliness of this scene that makes it poignant. It would be a pity to tame such a place, to repair it too neatly, to reinforce the gate, and to mend the broken parts; it would feel overly formal and lifeless.

I chuckle. My garden is full of mugwort and grass. Sei Shōnagon's words feel like a gentle nudge, a knowing wink across centuries. Perhaps a touch of wildness or imperfection is a necessary spice in the life of a woman living alone. Her wisdom rings true. "Overly formal and lifeless" is a state to be avoided. I wonder if this is a glimpse into her own heart, or a whisper of guidance to those of us navigating the quiet spaces of an empty nest. It's likely a combination of both, a timeless truth echoing through the ages.

A NEW FAMILY TRADITION: CHRISTMAS, YEAR TWO

It is already 7:00 PM when we finish dinner, but not dessert. "Mom, is it okay if we leave around 8:00? Maya asks, starting to load the dishwasher.

“Oh, no, that’s so soon. We still have to do some art and have dessert. Can you stay a little longer?” I plead. With a slight air of finality, Maya replies, “Okay, 8:30 then.” A tough girl.

Maya and her sweetheart Micah are back home from Toronto for winter break. This is our second annual collaborative painting, a tradition born from my desire to create lasting memories with these two bright, young people that I love so deeply. It is also a way to explore our relationship through a shared creative experience.

A large canvas sits on my dining table alongside acrylic paints, brushes, sponges, and various kitchen utensils I’d seconded as painting tools. Painfully aware of our tight timeframe—about an hour—I am both eager and apprehensive about the quality of outcome. It might be a total mess or something really rushed. However, in the spirit of collaboration, I reassure everyone (and myself), “There’s no such thing as a mistake!” I believe in the hidden potential of the process. I pose the question, “How should we approach this time? I am thinking abstract.” Splattering paint like Jackson Pollock is off limits, a boundary I unfortunately had to set to prevent accidental artistic messes on my dining furniture and floor.

We are leaning toward a more intuitive, feeling-led approach this time, unlike our concept-driven process last year. Micah’s intriguing question sets the tone: “Should we extend the shapes beyond the canvas, so the story continues in the viewer’s imagination?”

“Yes! I love that. It’s expansive and evocative,” I reply, recalling how artists often disregard the frame’s limitations.

Still, the pristine canvas presents a total sense of intimidation, making me feel a little daunted and challenged.

And then Maya says, "What if we try something like coffee-stain art? We could apply the paint randomly and then try attempting to discern emerging shapes or images." This sparks our creative direction. Micah then adds, "Let's each choose a colour for the first layer. I will count from three. Ready... three, two, one!" We all enthusiastically shout our choices: "Pink!" "Green!" "Purple!"

Beyond choosing a portrait orientation, we have no other plan. With our annual Studio Ghibli soundtrack playing, we dive in, applying freely our chosen colours to the blank canvas. It isn't intimidating since we are working together. I start spreading my pink using a brush; Maya, using a kitchen sponge, encroaches on my territory with her purple. Micah is busy applying his green with a serving knife. Our colours mingle and intertwine, creating a vibrant dance. We work in shared silence, deeply engrossed in our work. Our hands move with the tune.

Once the white canvas is nearly covered, we pause to share our senses. "What do you see?" we ask each other.

"I see light originating from the upper left and travelling diagonally."

"Yes, it resembles an explosion of light," I say. "Like a supercluster in the universe. Maya, that's a fantastic effect!" My pink remains visible beneath the dominant dark purple.

"I see a distinct line, almost like a coastline where the green and purple meet."

“Oh, I see it too! The green part feels really solid with those horizontal strokes.”

“It gives the impression of a mysterious sky looming over the land.”

“Exactly. The diagonal line effectively guides the viewer’s eye to the vibrant red area.”

We let our imaginations run wild, creating stories around the painting.

“It looks like a meteorite about to hit Earth.”

“Haha, it’s a dark theme, like today’s world.”

“Maybe it’s about climate change smoke reaching the sky or a nuclear explosion.”

“And yet, we see light breaking through the darkness.”

“Yeah, I feel this . . . like, life force at the end of that light, in the red part.”

Building on this shared understanding, Micah then poses a key question: “I like the dynamic diagonal movement. How can we make sure the second layer enhances this movement and directs the viewer’s gaze?”

I chime in, “Oh, you know, that painting from the Renaissance where the two fingers are almost touching—the creation scene, what’s it called again?”

Micah answers, “The Sistine Chapel.”

We stare at the painting for a while to see if anything jumps out at us. But now that I have that image of the two fingers in my head, I can’t see anything else. We keep looking.

Maya adds, “I like the diagonal idea. Using white to outline some images will create great contrast.”

Micah then suggests, "We could draw hands like in the Sistine Chapel. Or we could actually just draw any shapes with intention but without explaining them, just showing."

That idea of showing and not telling gives us a whole new focus. I get goosebumps; it is amazing and joyful to create something I never could have on my own.

I say, "What if we drew, like, part of a sphere, you know, like a snowflake crystal ball, to show another universe?"

Maya gets excited and says, "Yeah! Let's totally use that bright red part! How about we draw Saturn's rings in white and have that red explosion blasting right through them?"

The notion of a universe, or perhaps a hidden dimension, existing beyond or within our own captures our imaginations, resonating with Micah's earlier suggestion of transcending the confines of the canvas and the limitations of individual perspective. As we build layer upon layer of paint, we, both literally and figuratively, are building layers of meaning.

Now, using only white paint and a piece of string (from a Christmas gift ribbon!) as a makeshift compass, Maya and Micah carefully draw a partial circle, creating the illusion of a celestial body, or bubble, against the vibrant backdrop of our earlier work. Suddenly, it all starts to make sense, and we are all getting really excited. I then just go for it and splatter some white paint—carefully, but still kind of wild—breaking my own no splattering rule. This impulsive act splashes white speckles on my face. Micah kindly draws attention to this, adding to the shared laughter. And, by accident, I also splash some white drops along that diagonal line we saw at the beginning. Everything happens very quickly.

"Wow!" we exhale, captivated by the final image. We know, without a word, that the painting is finished. It is time for dessert.

I am entranced by this enigmatic collaborative process that saw the transformation of a blank canvas to a work of art in just an hour. Now I reflect on the interwoven meanings: the joy of creating together, the message conveyed by the completed artwork, and the deeper significance of our connection in that shared moment of creation.

See Beyond emerges as a potential title as it suggests this desire to transcend borders. Perhaps on a deeper level, I long to break free from my own habitual thinking and engage with the limitless potential I see in these young humans, to "see beyond" my own constraints. This act of co-creation has, to some degree, dissolved my ego. I feel a sense of boundless freedom, as if we are drifting through the cosmos together. The white speckles on my face are literal and figurative proof of this experience.

Did I actually "see beyond"? Later, Micah texts me, "It was a wonderful experience, and I felt like I've grown from just that one creative process."

Maya also tells me how much she enjoyed it. That is the perfect ending, a poignant reminder of Zeami's wisdom: cultivate art within the family, cherish fleeting moments, and pass down artistic expression.

The spirit of *Hidden Flowers* lives on.

A WOMAN AND "HANNYA"
watercolour,
9 × 12

The word *hannya* is derived from the Sanskrit word *prajñā*, which means "wisdom" or "knowledge." This connection suggests that the mask can also represent the wisdom gained through suffering and spiritual transformation.

EPILOGUE

Zuihitsu, a uniquely Japanese literary form often translated as "following the brush," blends non-fiction, musings, and even visual art into a spontaneous and layered text. It's a form of free-flowing expression in which thoughts meander and intertwine. Sei Shōnagon's *The Pillow Book*, a tenth-century masterpiece, is a perfect example. Her keen observations of daily life, like on those of a charming cat with its trailing leash, remind us to savour simple pleasures. This focus on the present moment resonates deeply with me, inspiring me to cultivate a similar awareness of beauty in the everyday.

In this spirit, I wrote the pieces in this book between the summer of 2023 and the winter of 2024, capturing moments of sadness, joy, and reflection amid my work with non-profits, teaching, and other commitments. This short book explores my first year of empty nesting and can be seen as a memoir of that transition. Writing became a way to explore my evolving understanding of life's meaning, a kind of flowering that brings joy and peace. And perhaps the most important lesson: nothing is final.

Reflecting back, I realize how deeply intertwined art and life have been in my life. Though no artist consciously directs the scene, I often sense a subtext of intrigue and sly indirection in the surface patterns and in the hidden depths that emerge when I pay attention.

The first year alone, without Maya, felt like an unscripted play, demanding perseverance yet rich with unexpected, joyful discoveries. Each unfamiliar corner revealed new possibilities. Initially unaware of my reserves of strength, I found support and inspiration from many. Everything, like a garden, has its time to ripen if tended patiently.

This year, for the first time, the raised bed in my front yard is filled with calendula. Thanks to my urban farmer-friend Marcel, it has become a personal oasis. Looking through my window at the vibrant yellow and orange flowers, side by side with collard greens and kale, brings me renewed appreciation for nature's wise momentum. These unexpected blooms revealed the forces at work: pollinators, rain, fertile soil—a perfect collaboration. Now, I observe myself, others, and the ebb and flow of life, and I am prepared for whatever emerges from soil, sun, and rain.

ACKNOWLEDGEMENTS

THIS BOOK OWES its existence to the support and encouragement of many individuals. I am especially grateful to my beta reader, colleague, and renowned filmmaker Daniel Conrad, whose insightful guidance, particularly on the power of "less is more," was invaluable. My heartfelt thanks also go to my dear friend, Joy Kogawa, one of Canada's most influential authors, best known for her novel *Obasan*, and whose wisdom and warm encouragement have sustained me over the years. And I extend my heartfelt gratitude to the community of friends, near and far, who have been an enduring source of inspiration and creativity. You know who you are.

My experience with Heritage House was a joy from start to finish. I am especially appreciative of my editor, Claire Mulligan, whose expert guidance and collegial demeanour rendered the process both enjoyable and inspiring. Claire's commitment to the development of

PUMPKIN'S REFLECTION
watercolour,
9 × 9

Who can truly know how Pumpkin perceives her reflection? Perhaps she sees a mirror image of her own joyful, kind, curious, and caring spirit. All those vibrant colours, surely, must reflect her radiant character.

authors is truly noteworthy. I also want to express my sincere gratitude to Lara Kordic, Associate Publisher; Kimiko Fraser, Publishing Assistant; Nandini Thaker, Editorial Manager, for her excellent editorial support; and the entire publishing team for their unwavering support.

Finally, I extend my heartfelt gratitude to my family. My daughter, Maya, has been a constant source of strength and hope. Maya's partner, Micah, and his family have enriched my life with their wisdom and kindness, and they have become cherished members of my own family. To my family in Japan, especially my father, Goro, and my sister, Haruko, and all my loved ones who have walked with me on this journey, thank you for your steadfast belief in me. And finally, my eternal love goes to my deceased grandparents, Konosuke and Tamiko, my uncles, Syunsuke and Tetsurō, and my mother, Yoko, my guiding star, whose love continues to illuminate my path.